WAKE UP AND LAUGH

WAKE UP AND LAUGH

THE DHARMA TEACHINGS OF
ZEN MASTER DAEHAENG

Daehaeng Kun Sunim

Foreword by Chong Go Sunim

Wisdom Publications
199 Elm Street
Somerville, MA 02144 USA
www.wisdompubs.org

Library of Congress Cataloging-in-Publication Data
Taehaeng, Sunim.
Wake up and laugh : the dharma teachings of Zen master Daehaeng / Daehaeng Kun
Sunim ; Foreword by Chong Go Sunim.
pages cm
Includes index.
ISBN 1-61429-122-5 (pbk. : alk. paper)
1. Religious life—Zen Buddhism. I. Title.
BQ9286.T34 2014
294.3'420427—dc23
                              2013028281

ISBN 978-1-61429-122-0
ebook ISBN 978-1-61429-145-9

21 20 19 18   4 3 2

Cover design by Philip Pascuzzo. Interior design by Gopa&Ted2, Inc. Set in Weiss Std 11/1.
Cover photo by Myong Hui Kim.

♻ This book was produced with environmental mindfulness. For more
information, please visit wisdompubs.org/wisdom-environment.

Wisdom Publications' books are printed on acid-free paper and meet the
guidelines for permanence and durability of the Production Guidelines for
Book Longevity of the Council on Library Resources.

Printed in the United States of America.

Please visit fcusa.org

Contents

Foreword

When I first saw Daehaeng Kun Sunim* in the summer of 1992, she was sitting on a porch, and it looked like she was quietly playing with the ants. Not quite the fierce image I had expected of a great Seon, or Zen, Master.

At the time I was in a graduate program, studying for a PhD I thought I needed, and had been practicing meditation for several years. I found meditation very helpful and revealing, providing many insights into life and who I was, but I seemed to have hit a wall. No matter what I did in my life and practice, I felt like I was chasing my tail.

Now I was sitting in the Dharma hall listening to Daehaeng Kun Sunim. Instead of being intense and intimidating, she seemed perfectly open and at ease, smiling as she looked around at us. It was a brutally hot July day and she was talking about many different

---

* At first introduction of a term, an asterisk indicates that this term can be found in the glossary.

things, most of which were new to me. Out of the blue I heard her say, "You have to search within yourself!"

I'd heard things like this before, but this time it was different. Those words reverberated throughout me; this was the next step I had been trying to figure out. It was as though I had been looking at a small piece of a painting for a long time, and now much of the surrounding painting was revealed.

Over the months that followed, as I listened to Daehaeng Sunim's teachings, I noticed a couple of interesting things. There were teachings I understood and those I didn't, but of the ones I understood, there wasn't anything that my experience showed me to be wrong. Further, of those teachings I didn't understand, if I just thought of them once in a while as I observed the world I lived in, they began to make sense to me. As I continue to practice, it becomes clear to me that her central teaching of letting go and trusting our inherent foundation, while appearing somewhat vague at the beginning, in the end truly becomes a great path to liberation.

The Dharma talks that comprise *Wake Up and Laugh* cover these and other essential teachings of Daehaeng Kun Sunim, from basic issues of how to engage in spiritual cultivation, to how to practice after awakening. In between she covers a variety of topics, such as how to free ourselves from destructive habits, common misunderstandings and pitfalls, and the beauty of a life lived while letting go of thoughts of "me." My hope is that you will discover for yourself what happens when you put these teachings into practice.

One last thing: a few years later I saw the video tape of that first

Dharma talk with Daehaeng Sunim, and nowhere in it did she say "You have to search within yourself." And yet I clearly heard her say it. It seems that not all Dharma talks are spoken with the mouth, and not all Dharma talks are heard with the ears.

Chong Go Sunim
Hanmaum International Culture Institute

Introduction

Faith in our true nature is the foundation of all of Daehaeng Kun Sunim's teachings. She saw this shining brightly within each of us and for over forty years taught people to make this inherent nature their focus.

In the Dharma talks that follow, she covers a vast range of topics and speaks to people at many different levels of practice and experience. At times she's speaking of things that are straightforward and easy to understand, and at other times she's speaking of things so far beyond our own experiences that they seem incomprehensible—but underlying all of this is faith in our true nature. Have faith in this inherent Buddha essence, entrust it with what arises in our life, and go forward while paying attention.

It doesn't matter that, in the beginning, we don't understand everything. If we just keep trying to apply the parts we do understand, spiritual experiences and understanding will naturally result, deepening our practice and spiritual life, and taking us on journeys we could never have imagined.

FAITH IN OUR TRUE NATURE

Within all of us is a great light, a treasure vast beyond imagining. Through this we are connected to all other beings; through this we are connected to all energy, ability, and enlightened beings. We can call this true nature, Buddha-nature, or God, but regardless of the name, it is inherently complete within us. And it is the source of our wisdom, energy, life force, and just about anything else you can think of.

Because this is the source of everything, this is what we must turn to, this is where we must look for our sustenance. This vast treasure is like the root that sustains and supports the tree. That root is where the tree has to look for its support. How long could a tree last if it didn't rely upon its root?

Although we all have our own root, many of us ignore it, trying to find sustenance and solutions outside of us. Instead, we have to discover how to draw upon the energy and wisdom that's already right there, waiting for us.

ENTRUSTING OUR TRUE NATURE WITH WHAT CONFRONTS US

Because this true nature is our root and our sustenance, this is where we need to place our faith and what we need to stand upon. We do this by entrusting it with the things that arise in our ordinary, mundane daily life: the small, the big, the good, the bad, the known, the unknown, and the confusing.

In the Dharma talks presented here, Daehaeng Kun Sunim gives several descriptions of the process of entrusting. In the very first talk, she compares this process to dying, because entrusting our true nature with something to which we've been clinging does feel a bit like dying. We have to open up and let go of it. We have to turn it over to something else, something other than the "me" that thinks it's in charge.

Further on, she compares the process of entrusting to putting scrap metal into a furnace. All we have to do is put the metal in, and the furnace will automatically return pure, clean metal. In this furnace, everything is melted down without distinction. There's nothing too big or too small for the furnace to melt down.

In another talk, she compares the process of entrusting to leaping over attachments and thoughts of "I" and "me," which are the source of our hindrances and difficulties. In so doing, we come to release the great energy and potential that's always been within us.

Ultimately, the process of entrusting is just returning things back to the place they came from. Everything arises from there, so that's the place they need to be returned to.

OBSERVING AND GOING FORWARD

"Must be present to win" is just as true for spiritual practice as it has been for thousands of raffles: we must be paying attention in order to notice the results of our thoughts and actions. Once we notice what happens, then we can begin to learn for ourselves. We can begin to see what happens when we entrust things, what happens when we let go, and what happens in response to the various thoughts we've given rise to. It's up to us to then take what we've noticed and apply it back to our life.

In addition to awareness, we must have effort. It takes work to overcome the momentum of millennia of habits, and we are the very ones who must make this effort. Our true nature isn't some outside force that will take care of things while we sit around; it's us at our most complete. When we do our best, and do it while entrusting the task to our Buddha-nature, it's as if our true nature meets us halfway and fills in the missing parts.

PUTTING IT ALL TOGETHER

The essence of all spiritual practice is discovering this divinity that's within each of us. It's there, but we aren't used to believing in it, nor are we used to relying upon it. So Daehaeng Kun Sunim teaches people to start by trying to rely upon this inner divinity, to start entrusting it with all the things that come up in life. And through this, we begin to get a sense of this inherent nature for ourselves. So have faith in this Buddha-nature, entrust it with what confronts you, and go forward, paying attention and taking care of things as best you can.

There are two other aspects of Daehaeng Kun Sunim's teachings that should be mentioned here, for these are essential for progress on any spiritual path: First, always view things positively. Because we are connected to everything in the universe, the thoughts we give rise to affect everything in our world. This may seem hard to believe, but our thoughts do truly create our world. Everything is inherently changing and manifesting every instant, but as we give rise to thoughts, those thoughts give direction and shape to that energy.

This closely relates to the second aspect: don't blame or criticize others. When we criticize people, we lock them in the shape of our critique, making it hard for them to change and for us to see who they truly are. We're also denying any role in what happened and ignoring our connection to the other person. That other person is fundamentally another shape of ourselves, and by ignoring this we turn our backs upon the nondual nature of reality. Be very careful about these two points—a negative outlook and a tendency to criticize others will do more harm to your spiritual path than just about anything else. This can't be emphasized enough: no matter how hard you are working on your spiritual path, your progress will remain stunted as long as you are caught up in these two behaviors.

As you read the Dharma talks that follow, take the parts that strike a chord with you and do your best to put them into practice. And take those parts that you don't understand and entrust them to your true nature, letting them percolate down within you. Later, understanding will come as you need those teachings and as your practice broadens. There are treasures beyond imagining here, waiting for you to remember them.

ABOUT DAEHAENG KUN SUNIM

Daehaeng Kun Sunim (1927–2012) was born in Seoul and is widely regarded as one of Korea's foremost Seon,* or Zen, masters. She awakened at a young age and spent the decades afterward applying what she experienced.

For many years she had struggled with the question of why people suffer. Daehaeng Kun Sunim realized that ultimately the answer was ignorance. People were unaware of the non-dual foundation that connects all existence. Unaware of this inherent connection, people lived as if they were disconnected from everyone else; unaware of the ever-changing nature of reality, people tried to grasp and immobilize that which is ever flowing. Unaware that their foundation is endowed with all of the ability of the universe, people thought themselves weak and helpless, limited to the kindness of others or the ability of their intellect.

Thus, people suffered because their behaviors and thoughts were not in harmony with the underlying truth of our world. And because people didn't know about this inherent foundation, with its infinite ability, they also didn't know how to free themselves from the suffering they had made.

So Daehaeng Kun Sunim began teaching people to entrust—to release—everything that confronts them to their inherent foundation and then to progress while observing. By continuing to apply and experiment with what we understand, a small grain of faith can grow into a great ball of flame that burns up all attachments and habits of the body and mind. Once this cloud of habits and discriminations has lifted, our inherently bright foundation, our true nature, can shine through.

While Seon masters have traditionally taught only monks and a few nuns, Daehaeng Kun Sunim was determined to teach spiritual practice in such a way that anyone, regardless of their occupation, gender, or family status, could practice and awaken.

With this in mind, in 1972 she established Hanmaum Seon Center as a place where everyone could come and learn about their true nature and how to live with freedom, dignity, and courage. And for the rest of her life, she taught only this.

To Discover Your True Self, "I" Must Die

SUNDAY, JULY 16, 1989

Although we are always truly functioning together as one, we also clearly exist as distinct individuals. In the midst of your busy lives, you have gathered here together to explore the path of truth, of how things really are. Thank you for this. When we gather like this, you, I, and all other beings are fellow practitioners and friends in the Dharma.

Today I'd like to begin by looking at what Shakyamuni Buddha said and did when he was born into this world. He said, "Throughout the heavens and the earth, there is nothing that is not this precious true self." Then he looked in the four directions and took seven steps. Buddhism appeared at that moment, and so did the practice of learning to rely upon our fundamental, true mind,* which is the path that leads to the discovery of our true self. Although I have never been to school, nor have I read many books, here is what I think the Buddha's actions mean.

First of all, what is the meaning of "Throughout the heavens and the earth, there is nothing that is not this precious true self"? I have always told you that your foundation is directly connected to the foundation of the universe and to the foundation of every single thing in your life. Even before the Buddha was born into this world, all beings were directly connected to each other through this foundation. Thus, if you awaken to this foundation, you can save all of the lives within your body, and you can also save all of the beings outside of your body. This is possible because all of these lives are connected to your foundation. You may have some questions about this, so let's discuss them at the end of the talk.

Second, what is the meaning of the Buddha looking in every direction? It means that the foundation is neither emptiness nor form, thus everything is able to operate and function together as a whole. The Buddha looked in the four directions to demonstrate this. Finally, his taking seven steps shows that even in the midst of this wholeness, you and I exist as distinct beings, and every single instant of our daily life is the path to the truth. The Buddha taught us this without using words, because this is something that can't be learned through words. The truth can never be learned through scholarship, intellectual knowledge, worldly power, fame, or theories. From the very beginning, practitioners have learned truth only by wisely investigating the fundamental questions of where we came from, where we are going, and how we should live.

These fundamental questions surround us. For example, we consist of earth, water, fire, and air. We live in the midst of these elements and sustain ourselves by eating them. You shouldn't ignore this. You should be thankful for those elements, because all living beings originated from them and have evolved from them into the life forms of today. Everything comes from them and returns to them. Everything disappears into them and then arises from them. This is the truth. A single flower petal hanging from a tree soon falls. If the petal is protected from the wind, it may hang there a little longer, but nonetheless, before long it too will fall.

Everything around us is no more permanent than drifting clouds. We have gathered here together because we all need to overcome the illusions of this realm. Our minds inherently embrace everything, without the least exception. Through this *Hanmaum,** this one mind, everything—plants, bugs, animals, and even inanimate objects—ceaselessly functions together. Although everything functions together as a whole, within this there is still clearly "you" and "me." But the very existence of "you" and "me" is empty, and in the midst of such emptiness, there exists one extraordinary thing. In order to discover it, we are cultivating mind together.

I always tell people who are new here, "First, you must die! Let go of everything and entrust everything!" But where do we let go to? We let go to our fundamental mind, our true nature. Because you exist, you experience all kinds of things. However, your fundamental mind is directly connected to the foundation of everything, so it's possible for you to take care of whatever you experience by entrusting it to your fundamental mind. It's like a power plant within you. This incredible power plant! If we need some energy, we can take out as much as we need. The energy of the power plant is infinite. No matter how much energy is taken out, its energy never decreases, and no matter how much energy is put in, it never overflows. The energy comes and goes; we just can't see it.

Therefore, daily life can be practicing Seon, or Zen. Just physically sitting down is not sitting in meditation. When your mind is at ease and you have let go of everything, this is sitting meditation and practicing Seon. However, this doesn't mean surrendering your firm, upright center of mind and just falling into emptiness. It is because you have this center that you are able to practice Seon and feel comfortable or uncomfortable. Without all of these feelings you could not attain wisdom or awaken to your true self, nor could you become a Buddha.

You should entrust everything that comes up in your life—solitude, poverty, loneliness, anxiety, illness—entrust this all to your foundation and live freely. Entrusting everything is letting go of attachments; it is the path of dying. "First, you must die!" means unconditionally letting go of everything, including what you understand and what you don't understand. It means letting go without clinging to reasons or excuses. When things go well, you should let go of them with gratitude. When things don't go well, you should also let go of them, knowing that "Nothing is fixed, so this situation too can change. My foundation, my true self, is the only one that can truly take care of all things. It will lead me safely along the path." Keep letting go like this. For it is only by dying unconditionally that you can discover your true self, your eternal root.

Second, you must die again. While practicing here, some of you have discovered yourself. Yet you still have not discarded your habits and thoughts of "I," "me," and "mine." So you're thrilled if a

Buddha appears in your dreams but worried if you see a ghost. And when you feel or experience something extraordinary, you carelessly talk about that experience. What you're seeing and hearing are just illusions, but nevertheless you're clinging to them. This is why you must die again.

Now do you understand why first you must die and keep what you experience to yourself, and why you must die yet again, keeping what you experience secret? Even though you are able to see or know certain things after you discover your true self, those powers are not the Way. Even if you have obtained the five subtle powers— the abilities to know another's thoughts and feelings, to know past and future lives, to hear anything, to see anything at any place, and to appear anywhere without moving your body—this is still not the Way. Only when you are free from attachment to those subtle powers will you be the master of them and able to use them to help all beings. Revealing what you hear, see, or know will only bring trouble. First, it will cause trouble for the Buddhadharma; second, it will cause trouble for the temple; and third, it will cause trouble for you. Once you discover yourself, you enter the stage of experimenting. Know that what you experience while awake and while dreaming are all your true self teaching you. And keep everything you learn secret.

Even though you may be able to see, hear, or know things that others are unaware of, do it without clinging to any thought of "I see," "I hear," or "I know," and do not reveal to others what you experience. At this stage of practice, you need to experiment with what you have learned. Your experiments will result in experiences, and then you should try to put those experiences into action. This is a very powerful stage of practice, so you must be careful to die a second time and keep what you experience to yourself.

If you keep everything secret and can completely let go of the five subtle powers, you will eventually be able to control them. If you're a slave to your body, how can you take care of it and keep it healthy? Likewise, you must be able to free yourself from the five subtle powers. Although you see what others can't see, release it. Although you hear what others can't hear, release it. Although you know others' minds and past lives, release all of that. Although your body is able to transcend time and place, and instantly go anywhere, you should also release that. This is keeping it secret. This is the very way to realize the truth of how mind works and attain wisdom. It is like a secret path where, through application and experiencing, you thoroughly understand this fundamental mind and become able to use it as needed. This secret gateway is inside of you. It is within you, working through your five senses. Don't go looking for the entrance somewhere else. Discover the truth through the door that is already within you.

Third, you must die yet again. If you can keep what you experience secret and free yourself from all attachments to the five subtle powers, then at that point, even though you and others clearly exist as distinct beings, discriminations and barriers between yourself and others will utterly disappear. At this stage, you will be able to manifest such that you become others, and others become you. Your ability to respond and manifest will become so powerful.

What is manifesting? Because mind has no form, an infinite variety of different shapes can come out from it. This is called the hundred and ten billion manifestation bodies of Buddha, because Buddha responds to you as you request: If you want the mountain god, Buddha manifests as the mountain god. If you want Avalokitesvara,* the Bodhisattva of compassion, Buddha manifests as Avalokitesvara. And so Buddha manifests to everyone differently. Furthermore, Buddha responds not only with physical forms but also with compassion and warmth.

Buddha manifests, transforms, and responds to every single life. Such manifestation is Buddha's stepping down from the realm of the Buddhas for the sake of unenlightened beings and working as a Bodhisattva.* This is the same compassionate action of the Lotus-Flower Buddha, the Medicine Buddha, and of Samantabhadra* Bodhisattva. Buddha responds to everyone. Regardless of who they are—the spirit of a tree or the spirit of the earth, man or woman, rich or poor, old or young, someone with power or without power, intelligent or unintelligent—Buddha responds equally to them all. This is what it means to be a Buddha.

These three stages of dying again and again can be thought of as the process of perfecting a human being. However, this isn't the completion of "me"; instead, it is where everything has been combined together and works as a whole. You still flow as yourself, and I flow as myself, yet in the midst of this, the whole, as Buddha, responds as needed. In this way, you can become anyone. According to the need, their eyes can become your eyes, and their hands can become your hands. Because you are one with them, you can understand their circumstances. Because you are one with them, you can truly know their pain. This is the compassion of Buddha, manifesting in a hundred and ten billion different forms. However, which manifestation is truly Buddha? Is it when Buddha takes the form of a worm? Is it when Buddha appears in front of you as Avalokitesvara? How about when Buddha manifests as a dog? You can't truly call any of these "Buddha"; Buddha is always changing.

Always changing and flowing every single moment is the Way, and is truth itself. If anything is "attained," it is the path that transcends all names and labels, the truth called "supreme, unsurpassed enlightenment." This path and truth are what the word "Buddha" means.

If we follow the path that the Buddha taught, we will be able to go forward intelligently, with faith grounded in our true nature. Here "intelligently" means releasing everything to your true self, your foundation, and not letting yourself be disturbed by anything. Seon Master Baizhang* was teaching this when he said, "You must not dig the ground, nor not dig the ground. Why is this?" Master Baizhang also said, "When you truly understand this practice, you will be able to plant and harvest, and feed all sentient beings with one bowl of food. Further, no matter how much you give, that bowl will never be emptied." The Buddha and countless awakened masters have also said the same thing and led us toward this path. They came to this world and, while doing without any trace of doing, showed us the path to the truth.

When the Buddha held up a lotus flower before the assembly, only the disciple Kassapa* understood and replied with a smile. He smiled because his mind had become one with the Buddha.

Through this exchange the Buddha was saying, "To you, I transmit this truth, the enlightenment that is not enlightenment." He did this in order to show us that understanding the Dharma is more than words alone. To use a Korean expression, "if you hit the wall, the roof should shake." Hearing just one phrase, you should try to understand the unspoken, underlying meanings.

For example, when people hear the word "light," they tend to think of only the bulb and the switch. There's no awareness of the electricity coming and going. People only notice that the light comes on when they flip the switch. Similarly, people don't perceive where they came from or where they're going; they only see the bulb and the fixture. However, if you can see the electric power, then you'll better understand how the bulb and fixture work.

The most important thing is this: First, you must let go of everything and die, and keep what you experience secret. Second, you must let go of everything and die again, and not reveal what you experience. Third, you must die yet again and keep what you experience secret. Then you'll be able to attain wisdom and respond as a manifestation of the Dharma. Without dying like this, you won't be able to reach the point where the entire universe bursts forth from within you.

All of the learning we've done since childhood, the schooling, the reading, the work experience, and learning to adjust to the patterns of society, has been a lot of hard work, hasn't it? However, none of this effort has been in vain. After you've realized the essence of your mind, you'll discover that everything you've ever learned, even the ordinary knowledge, will be useful. It will all be helpful because worldly learning and what we learn through our fundamental mind are not separate. Neither can be thrown away; both are necessary.

Then what comes first? You all have the mind that exists before the occurrence of thoughts. This mind is called Buddha-nature and has many other names. I am always telling you that, within your body, some lives are inclined toward good and some are inclined toward harmful things; sometimes these lives make you suffer and sometimes they make you happy. But don't be deceived by them. These lives, these karmic consciousnesses,* keep causing all kinds of trouble and suffering. However, your true self, your center, is complete as it is. Your true self is upright and powerful. It is brightness itself.

Nonetheless, you tend to become worried and think negatively if, for example, you have a disturbing or strange dream. This indicates that you are not so good at handling your thoughts. When you're thinking negatively, feeling sad or depressed, you should promptly change your thoughts, thinking, "Those feelings and thoughts all arise from Juingong,* our true essence, so it's also Juingong that can keep those kinds of feelings and thoughts from arising." Do this and your state of mind will change before long. And yet people keep telling me things like "I feel depressed" or "I'm sick" while clinging to these thoughts. Why do they tell me these things? The one who can take care of everything is you yourself. The "you" that is your true nature can deal with whatever arises, in whatever form!

By the way, you should know that when we seek the Dharma, it's often necessary to ask questions of each other and discuss spiritual practice. When fellow practitioners gather, it's good for them to energetically discuss all aspects of practice and their understanding, free of excessive politeness or fear of criticism. Paying attention to other people's experiences and observing how they act can help you a lot. From other's experiences you can learn many things: "I should be careful not to do that" or "That's a good way to do it," and so forth. In this way, you can gain wisdom and even come to understand exactly what you have to do. Some of you may be thinking, "You said that we have to let go of everything and rely upon our fundamental mind, but now you're saying that we have to work in the realm of speech and discussions?" People often wonder about this, so I'll say something about it now.

When you're looking for an answer, when you're asking a question, open yourself up and do it from your fundamental mind. When you ask me a question, I'm absorbing your words and that energy, and when I speak to you, you're hearing my words and also absorbing that energy. All of those words have been absorbed, haven't they? Asking questions and having discussion like this, while relying upon your fundamental mind, can really help you deepen and broaden yourself.

Our fundamental mind can communicate with and connect to anything. It has no physical form, so it can become any form of energy, such as light, electricity, or magnetic energy. Because of this, each side automatically absorbs what is said. When this side speaks, that side absorbs it, and when that side speaks, this side absorbs it. Like electricity or a wireless phone, mind communicates without any trace of coming or going. All of this is the working of the profound Dharma. Where is this profound and mysterious Dharma? It's in every part and every instant of our daily life. As I said before, when I have absorbed what you've said, and when you have absorbed what I've said, everything's gone, no traces remain at all.

However, as the Buddha told us, in the midst of this fleeting life, where everything ceaselessly flows and changes, there is one thing that is eternal. Physical things change every moment, but their root lasts forever. We're cultivating our minds in order to realize the eternal essence of this root, and so live freely. If you truly understand that the foundation of your mind is directly connected to the foundation of the universe, you will be able to truly hear, see, and evaluate everything throughout all visible and invisible realms. For these abilities are inherent within our foundation.

If you heard about something completely new, something you'd never even imagined, you'd probably think that it was nonsense. However, it is not nonsense to say that the foundation of human beings' minds and the foundation of everything in the universe are directly connected. Your foundation is connected to the foundation of everything you encounter in the world. Pay attention to the world around you and see how things work. People tend to gather together according to similar karmic affinity, and fit themselves to the group's rhythm. But life in that group isn't always pleasant, is it? When people don't know about this fundamental connection, they speak harshly to each other and fight. For them, life is a war, although they don't realize it.

The last time I went to the United States, a group of Protestants and Catholics invited me to give a talk. Although we came from different cultures and religious backgrounds, I had no problem communicating with them. Why? Because the Korean word for Buddhism, Bulgyo, is not just the name of a certain group or organization. The first syllable, *bul*, means the eternal foundation and source of life, through which everything is interconnected. Because each one of us has this foundation of life, we have been able to evolve up to the level of human being, and will be able to become great spiritual beings like the Buddha. The second syllable, *gyo*, means words of truth and the teachings about life. This is like the wisdom and life experiences that a parent shares with his or her children. Thus, Buddhism, or Bulgyo, refers to everything in the world. It encompasses everything.

There are so many religions in this world besides Christianity, Judaism, Hinduism, Islam, and Buddhism. But in almost all of them, people believe in supreme beings that exist outside of and apart from themselves. Wherever I've gone, I've seen people blindly following images, names, or specific persons. But this can't lead us to what's true and essential. The Buddha taught us that the path to truth is within ourselves, saying, "Discover your fundamental mind, and in so doing, be able to perfectly take care of whatever arises and experience a truly worthwhile life. Escape forever from the cycle of birth and death, transcend time and place, and realize the truth of the universe."

I often ask myself if I am doing everything I can to guide people in the right direction. Am I living up to my name, Daehaeng, which means "Great Actions of a Bodhisattva?" I'm often checking to see if there is some aspect or wiser way of taking care of things that I've overlooked. Sometimes I feel like a bright gem, but other times I feel small and worthless. Sometimes when I go for a walk, if I see a twig, I become that twig. Sometimes when I see how people and animals live, I find myself smiling. Other times my eyes are filled with tears.

The awakened masters of old used to wear bells on their shoes when they passed through tall grass and brush, and even during heavy rainstorms, they walked slowly and steadily. Why did they do so? They wore bells because they did not want to accidentally kill even a tiny life, and they took steady steps because they were always focused on the unwavering, fundamental mind. You may already know this, but if you live without any kind of self-reflection, the days fly by and before you know it, your time here is finished.

So regardless of whether you are walking, driving, or working, always remember what's really doing all those things. Relying on your fundamental mind guides you to the correct path and allows you to free yourself and live harmoniously with your neighbors, while fulfilling your obligations. Relying upon your fundamental mind will also guide you during your future lives, for it is the act of watering your root.

Let me answer your questions today. When you ask questions, ask without any thought of asking. No matter what kind of problem you face, you should first return it inwardly, then the solution will arise. Likewise, when you want to say something, first return it inwardly, and then speak. By doing so, your anxiety will disappear and you will be composed, without rashness. Go ahead and ask whatever you want, but don't make up a question. Rather, ask naturally. Even though you feel like you didn't express yourself well, don't feel bad. Feel free to say anything. That is how I speak. It's nice when things are natural.

We're here to learn about "doing without any thought of doing," so just ask without worrying about anything. Your questions will be helpful for everyone. If you come forward here and ask questions, those will become spiritual food for everyone's practice and will help guide everyone toward the truth.

QUESTIONER 1: I have been praying for all sentient beings ever since I started coming to the Seon Center. But I wonder if I have been practicing correctly. Although you tell us to let go of everything completely, whenever I recite the name of Ksitigarbha* Bodhisattva, my heart aches and my eyes fill with tears. Sometimes I ask myself, "Could I become Ksitigarbha Bodhisattva? No, how could I?"

KUN SUNIM: You said that you often seek out Ksitigarbha Bodhisattva. However, you can discover Buddha regardless of the name you use. "Buddha-nature" is a name. "Ksitigarbha" is a name, and "Juingong" is also a name. All of these are just names. If you think that Ksitigarbha is great and superior to you and that you can find Ksitigarbha outside of yourself, then this is a delusion. It's completely useless. If you seek outside of yourself, you may also develop some severe psychological problems. Ksitigarbha refers to the treasure within you, the Buddha-nature that is hidden by ignorance,* by darkness. Therefore, never seek it outside of yourself. If you are always attracted to outside things, you will be far from finding your true self. Furthermore, you won't be able to properly take care of your family or yourself.

This Buddha-nature can also be known by names other than "Ksitigarbha," because Buddha-nature is the source of everything and encompasses everything. Because all things are combined together and continuously work together as a whole, Buddha-nature can be called "Juingong" or "my inner Juingong." Juingong includes every blade of grass and every single insect; here everything operates as one mind within a house made of earth, water, fire, and air. Because of this center, because of this treasure, your consciousness functions, and so does your good and bad karma, which are gathered together with your center. So stop reciting just the name of Ksitigarbha. Stop letting yourself be drawn outwardly. Know that everything functions because of Juingong. And don't forget that Juingong, Buddha-nature, and Ksitigarbha all exist within you.

When I was in New York the last time, people were freely asking questions. There was even the question "Do we live to eat or do we eat to live?" Someone beside me grumbled that it was a stupid question, but I disagreed, because it gave me a chance to address an important point. I used my glass of water as an example. If you're hot and thirsty, you open the refrigerator and go straight for the cool water. When you are dying of thirst, do you first ask yourself whether you drink water to live or you live to drink water? No, of course not. When you're thirsty, you go straight for the water. This is also how we should practice relying upon our fundamental mind.

Likewise, there is nothing wrong with whatever you ask. Go ahead and ask about the things you don't understand. But it's also okay to check your understanding, to ask about what you understand, for your question may help other's practice. When people read books, they tend to get caught up in the meaning of the words, without thinking of the blank paper underlying the words. People pay attention only to the letters on the paper. So, in order to know the blank paper, let's ask questions.

QUESTIONER 2: I'm so grateful to be able to meet you today. I've been a Buddhist for twelve years. I would like to ask you about a term I've heard a lot about. What is the Saha world, the Sahalokadhatu?

KUN SUNIM: The Saha world is the very place where you are living right now, the world we human beings live in. This place where we are sitting is the Saha world. To explain it another way, north, south, east, and west are all the Saha world. There are lots of different ways the meaning of "Saha world" can be expressed. Everything is within the realm we live in, in the middle of our daily life, not anywhere else. We need to think deeply about what this means, and what it means in regard to how we can follow the teachings of the Buddha, how we can cultivate self-sustaining faith, and how our body, our family, and children can live freely, without ever being caught in the cycle of birth and death.

QUESTIONER 3: Until I met you, I had practiced the teachings and mantras of one of the new religions that have arisen in Korea. Some of its teachings are about living an altruistic life and dissolving resentments. Altruistic living means saving myself and others, which seems similar to the teaching of Buddhism—saving other beings is the same as saving myself. "Dissolving resentments" refers to the resentments that people have made since the beginning of mankind, the resentments that have permeated even heaven. It means saving not only all the living beings in the present, but also dissolving the resentments that exist in the invisible realm. Also, I heard that heaven consists of nine realms, and that Buddhas and Bodhisattvas reside in the seventh heaven, while the founder of this movement resides in the ninth heaven, the highest of all. And...

KUN SUNIM: Look, in a nutshell, if they say that he's in heaven, then he's not there. Heaven is not heaven, and the earth is not the earth. Heaven and the earth do not exist separately. Everything depends upon our minds. People who say that they have the ability to save others cannot actually save anyone. People who can truly save don't talk about it. If your son were drowning now, you'd dive straight in and save him. You wouldn't waste time talking about it. You'd just do it without saying anything, without any thought of "I will" or "I did." Even though someone talks again and again about saving people, those words are all just theories.

So instead of relying upon other people's power, know yourself first. Even if Shakyamuni Buddha were here right now, don't place your faith in his physical form. Place your faith in your own fundamental mind. Do this and discover it; awaken, attain wisdom, and save the lives within your own body. Unless you can do this, you won't be able to save the lives outside of your body.

QUESTIONER 3: I see.

KUN SUNIM: You must know yourself first. If you didn't exist, could others exist? Could religions exist? Could there be a theory that someone is in heaven? It doesn't matter to me whether they say someone is in heaven or not. That's their opinion. However, what I want to say to you is that only after you discover your true self will you be able to know the essential teachings of your religion and whether he is really in heaven or not. If you don't know such things for yourself, if you haven't experienced them, how can you talk about those things? People have to know how to awaken to what's already within themselves. So telling them things like "Place your faith in me, I'll save you. I'm a heavenly being" is inexcusable. In helping people I'm just running errands for them; my only concern is how to do this properly and how to avoid disgracing the Buddhadharma. So my hope is that you will know yourself first.

QUESTIONER 3: I will try to know myself first.

KUN SUNIM: Good. I'm sorry if I seemed a bit harsh.

QUESTIONER 4: It is an honor to meet you today for the first time. I've had a question in my heart for a long time, and I hope you can answer it. A while ago, you told us that the source of all afflictions is ignorance. But I am not sure what ignorance means. I'd be grateful if you would explain this for me.

KUN SUNIM: When we say *ignorance* we mean "lack of light" or "darkness." Like the soil that covers a tree's roots, all of the karmic consciousnesses we've created over countless lives keep us from seeing our own root, our own true self. They are recorded within us, and it's these consciousnesses that lead us to be reborn; so, in our lives, ignorance begins with birth. Because of this ignorance, because people don't see their true self, they're called "unenlightened beings."

Even though I do not explain things well or I mispronounce some words, please understand what I meant to say!

How wonderful it is to gather like this!

QUESTIONER 5: I've been studying Buddhism for a long time, and recently one of my friends converted to another religion. When we meet and have a drink, we often argue with each other. I think he would be able to help many people if he were to learn your teachings, so I usually try to talk him into coming to the Seon Center. So we often have friendly quarrels.

Every morning and evening, and every night before I go to bed, I pray, "Oh, great, holy, compassionate Buddha and our Kun Sunim, the living Buddha! I am filled with deep gratitude. Through the Buddha's compassion let me have a grateful mind and repay the kindnesses done to me, and let me lead my life harmoniously.

Through this let me know and experience my true self, Juingong, so that I can help other sentient beings as well as my family." I pray and chant this three times a day while trying to find my true self, my Juingong. But it doesn't seem to work. So I asked my friend about it.

So he said, "Why do you trouble yourself by bowing to Kun Sunim and the image of Buddha? Isn't that idol worship? You yourself have criticized others for behaving like that!" So I replied, "How can it be idol worship to bow to Kun Sunim? She is a living Buddha, not a statue. I bow to Kun Sunim at home and even while walking. " He said again, "If you think so, you're badly mistaken. That's idol worship. Go and ask Kun Sunim whether or not you are practicing correctly. Ask her." We argued about this a few days ago.

KUN SUNIM: Today's questions are raising so many important points. In the future, let's make sure there's always time for questions after the Dharma talks.

I think your friend is right. Haven't I said these things many times already? Never abandon your upright center. Don't blindly believe in things or let yourself become a slave. And don't bow to me. When you are bowing, you are not bowing to me or to the Buddha, but to your own self. I've always told you that the Buddha statue is your own image, that the Buddha's mind is your mind, and that your very life is the Buddha's life. When you understand this, your one bow can become ten thousand bows. One bow can become three bows, or it can become seven bows. It's completely up to you. It depends entirely upon how you use your mind.

So don't pray to me. If you raise up something and pray to it, it becomes a thing apart from yourself. Have faith in your true self, in Juingong, and entrust the situation with your friend to it. Don't be caught up in whether or not he comes here. You might think that it would be nice if he comes here, but this is your idea, not his. Each person follows the path that seems best for her or him, because each person's level is different. Now, a drinking glass can hold no more than a glassful. Even a barrel can hold no more than a barrelful. However, look at the ocean. It holds all the waters of the sea, and still it can receive everything that comes to it. Like this, everyone is living according to their own capacity, and every single thing has value and its place. Nothing is worthless. When you go to the store, you can see that cups are displayed with cups, bowls are displayed with bowls, and plates are displayed with plates. This is also true of human beings.

Because things work this way, if you truly want to guide your friend, you shouldn't pray to some object or person saying, "Please make him do this." Instead, just smile and let go of the situation with a calm mind, knowing, "My Juingong understands everything and can guide my friend. Since my Juingong and his Juingong are not separate, everything can be communicated through this foundation." Don't pray to certain places or things. You should not place a Buddha statue in your house and bow to it, nor should you place a bowl of water, incense, and candles in front of it and offer up prayers. If you keep praying to be saved by something outside yourself, this becomes a habit. It will cause difficulties for your children and will follow you even after death.

When there's something you have to take care of, or something you want, completely release it. With faith, let go of everything to this fundamental place and always rely upon it in all your activities. Then what you've entrusted will silently manifest into the world. For example, one day your friend may say, "Hey, why don't you take me to your temple? I'd like to go there." Everything should be done naturally like this, without forcing it. We gathered here voluntarily. Nobody forced us. You came here because you wanted to come here, right? Long ago, a dying man wanted to take his money with him. Just then, the money said, "You spent your life following me because it was you who loved me. I wasn't the one who loved you, so I'm not going to follow you now." In particular, issues of religion and faith cannot be forced.

We have to believe in our own guide. This guide is our fundamental mind, the mind that exists before we are even born, and which is vastly more than what we normally think of as our mind. Having faith in your fundamental mind is like filling an automobile with the fuel that makes it run. This energy is so plentiful! Not only is there enough for you, there's more than enough to give to others as well. Thus, believe in your Juingong, which is within you, and entrust everything to it. Just peacefully release everything. Then your practice will be well on its way.

There are so many difficult things in life, so isn't it nice that we sit together like this and discuss and exchange ideas about how to cultivate our minds?

QUESTIONER 6: This is the first time I've had a chance to meet you in person, but I've had many talks with you through your books. In those books, you told us to let go of everything, and I have tried to do so ever since. As I keep practicing, fundamentally it seems that what I have to let go of is my own ego, the sense of "me," rather than the things that happen to me. However, the more I think about letting go of myself, the tighter I seem to hold on.

Every time I reread your books, different aspects really touch my heart. I feel that if I just keep reading these books, I'll be able to thoroughly grasp Juingong for myself. Yet, since I'm able to meet you today, I'd like to ask you about something. I think I haven't made great progress in my practice because my faith is weak. So I would appreciate it if you would tell me how I can make my faith stronger.

KUN SUNIM: I think your question will help everyone here. Some people say to me, "Sunim, how can we live if we release everything?" And you say that the more you try to release, the tighter you hold on. Yet where are those words that you said? They're already gone, aren't they? That's it itself! Right now we are living just like that—naturally releasing everything at every single moment. Is there actually anything that you can hold on to or anything that you can let go of? No, there isn't. This releasing is very natural and yet, at the same time, something that can be very hard to do.

So I can well imagine why an ancient Seon master said the following: "If the Buddha hadn't taken seven steps, looked in all directions, and said, 'Throughout the heavens and the earth, there is nothing that's not this precious true self,' then he wouldn't have caused all these disturbances. If I had been there, I would have killed him and thrown his body to the dogs." He said this because we've already let go of everything. Life is changing instant by instant, with nothing to grasp on to. The very essence of life is letting go. When you met your son just a moment ago and said goodbye, the moment is already gone. It's been let go of. But even "letting go" is just a name, a word, and a theory. Our living itself is just flowing, with nothing to cling to or let go of. Everything just passes by. We encounter so many things and do so many things and are always moving on to something else. Could you take all of this and show it to someone? No. This is what I'm talking about.

Therefore, there is nothing to grasp, and nothing to not grasp. As Seon Master Baizhang said, "You should neither dig nor not dig. You should neither greet nor not greet. Yet within this, there is something special. Do you know what it is?" Another Seon master once said, "There is something essential that gives you thirty blows if you come in and thirty blows if you go out. What is it?" In another case, someone asked a Seon master, "Where is Buddha?" The master told him to come close and then grabbed his collar and began hitting him with a cane. The man cried out, "Ouch! Ouch! Ouch!" and the master shouted at him, "Where is this 'Ouch!' coming from?!"

If you think deeply about this, you may realize that developing deep faith in your true self is most important. With faith, you can let go. Without faith, you can't let go. Why can't people believe in their true self? They believe in others so easily, but why don't people believe in themselves? Whether you're a great person or not, whether you're skilled or not, that which has made you this way is you. So start with yourself! Who else can take your place on your deathbed? Can anyone be sick instead of you? Can anyone sleep for you? Can anyone eat for you? Can anyone else go to the bathroom for you? You have to believe in your true self, that which leads and moves you; what else could you take refuge in? With faith in your Juingong, just let go of everything. No matter how difficult a thing you face, release it completely to your true self, knowing, "Juingong can solve even this." All we have to do is let go. So let go and then observe how things develop. By watching how things go, you'll have experiences. Experiment with those, try to apply them and put them into practice. This is how you can discover your true self, awaken, and attain wisdom.

Don't think of anything as separate from yourself. For example, in praying to someone or something, there is a strong tendency to see that which hears your prayers as existing apart from yourself. Therefore I never tell people to pray to Buddha. If they pray to Buddha, Buddha becomes something apart from themselves. I'm not saying that I don't believe in Buddha. It's just that so many people have, over the course of many lifetimes, developed the habit of thinking that things are separate from themselves. When they chant "Ksitigarbha" or "Avalokitesvara," they tend to look up to them and see those Bodhisattvas as apart from themselves. Why do they do that? So I tell people not to call out to Buddha or God and to instead believe in their foundation, the one that is doing all things. I do this because I want everyone to be able to go forward together, and each to be able to walk on his or her own two feet. So I hope that all of you will reflect upon what I have said today, have strong faith, and release everything! As I said before, our natural state is letting go and moving forward.

QUESTIONER 7: When our society has so many urgent problems, how can I let go of everything unconditionally? What will become of our society if we release everything? It seems to me that if I release everything, I'll sleep all day long.

KUN SUNIM, laughing: You asked an interesting question, but what you are thinking of is not what the Buddha taught us. What you are talking about is called "falling into emptiness." Do you understand the difference? The reason the Buddha taught us about letting go and going forward is so that we could know the true meaning of life and feel the worth of life, so that we could live uprightly by seeing both sides, the invisible realm and the visible realm, each of which is fifty percent of the whole. Does this sound like sleeping all day long?

And you're already letting go of everything. What has happened to all of the things you've felt, done, and experienced over just the last twenty-four hours? Can you show any of those to me? No, they're gone; you've already let go of them.

QUESTIONER 7: I can't show them to you, but I can remember them, so they must exist within my mind, don't they?

KUN SUNIM: Listen, I'm not saying that you don't have thoughts or memories, or that you don't do anything. It's natural to think about and take care of the things that come up in your life. I've never said, "Don't make money, don't participate in society, don't fall in love, don't do anything at all." Just understand that everything is already flowing, and don't try to cling to it. Nothing remains stationary and unchanging.

Think about how many people you meet in just a single day. First you come across one person and then another. You're never continuously meeting only the same person, are you?

QUESTIONER 7: No.

KUN SUNIM: Right. Even the things you hear are always different, aren't they?

QUESTIONER 7: There are some books and people who say that the world has certain rules, and that if we follow those, we can take care of most of the problems of society, and even free ourselves.

KUN SUNIM: Look! Don't talk about theories. People who follow this path, people who explore the truth, don't waste their time on theories.

QUESTIONER 7: But you said that blind faith is rather dangerous.

Without having experienced enlightenment, how can someone like me believe unconditionally, without any doubt?

KUN SUNIM: Blind faith in others is dangerous! What I'm trying to tell you is to believe in yourself. Why can't you believe in yourself? You're the one who walked over here, right?

QUESTIONER 7: Well, yes.

KUN SUNIM: Can you believe the fact that you walked over here?

QUESTIONER 7: It is true that I walked over here, but...

KUN SUNIM: Then, can you believe that you're the one who is doing everything else in your life?

QUESTIONER 7: Yes.

KUN SUNIM: Your mind knows this fact, but you can't show it to anyone else because mind has no form. But you're aware of it nonetheless, right?

QUESTIONER 7: Yes.

KUN SUNIM: So what I'm telling you to do is find the fundamental mind that underlies all those thoughts. To do this, believe in your inner foundation, and entrust everything to it. It's within you and is capable of taking care of everything. If you keep entrusting like this, then what you're doing will function in the invisible realm and will eventually manifest into the visible realm. It's like this: if you eat something, later it will automatically come out, without you needing to think about the process. When you're hungry, you eat something. Later you start to feel pressure inside and so go sit on the toilet, and then something comes out. This process also describes how the things we input to our foundation manifest into the world; however you look at it, it is the truth, it is natural, it is science.

QUESTIONER 7: Do you mean that we should live only by following our natural impulses?

KUN SUNIM: Of course not! Listen, if you just ask questions without reflecting inwardly, how can you make any progress? Instead of immediately asking others, entrust your questions to your foundation. Right now within your body, there are trillions of lives working together, with each doing its own job. All of these lives exist together with you, and every single one of them is connected and communicating through your foundation. So start by trusting this foundation, your foundation, with everything that arises in your life. Start by doing this, and you'll be able to take care of your own body.

QUESTIONER 7: Unconditionally?

KUN SUNIM: Yes, unconditionally.

QUESTIONER 7: You mean that we should entrust all of our worries to this foundation, such as worries about myself, my family, and the people around me?

KUN SUNIM: If you have faith in your unseen, true self, and entrust everything to it, it will all be taken care of harmoniously.

Through this fundamental mind, all things are connected. So when you release something to it, what you've released is evaluated and communicated to everything. For example, in your body, the cerebrum, cerebellum, spinal cord, and all parts of your body are all connected and communicating with each other. So when you entrust something to your foundation, that thing is communicated throughout your body, because all those parts are connected together. If you can understand just this aspect, you will be able to understand everything. So don't cling to reasons or explanations. Just entrust everything to your true self. Okay?

Are there any more questions? No? We've been here for a long time and your legs probably hurt from sitting so long, so let's call it a day. Before we finish, I would like to repeat one thing.

Awakened masters sometimes said, "Discard everything! Let go of everything! There is nothing to attain." But later they also said, "There's not a single thing to discard." Within these two different phrases, there was something extraordinary that couldn't be expressed with words. To try to communicate it, some masters took a staff and hit the floor, some raised one finger, others thrust out a fist, while still others shouted "Ha!" All of those actions were showing that this extraordinary thing was right there.

Take what I've said here today and use it to discover what this extraordinary thing is.

The Furnace within Yourself

SUNDAY, SEPTEMBER 17, 1989

YOUR FOUNDATION IS DIRECTLY CONNECTED
TO EVERYTHING

Today we are here together again to discuss the cultivation of mind. When I talk to you, you absorb that, and nothing remains. When you talk to me, I absorb it, and again nothing remains. This is the principle of "doing without any thought of doing."

It seems to me that some people have become a little bit lost about how to cultivate mind. They argue among themselves, saying, "In this temple we're practicing Mahayana Buddhism," and "No, it's Theravada Buddhism." Still others complain that things in the temple don't seem to be run very systematically. Although at a glance things may seem disorganized, once you begin to understand the principle of one mind for yourself, you'll realize that truth—the way that everything functions—is very systematic.

Today we are learning how to make our daily life Seon and how to make it accord with the truth itself. In order to explore our minds, we are learning to make everything—including sitting, standing, and lying down—part of our Seon practice. We are also learning that there is no distinction between sitting meditation, standing meditation, and lying meditation. In other words, practicing Seon includes all of the things that you generally need to do in your daily life—keeping order in society, maintaining a sense of morality, loving others, keeping your word, and upholding trust. In this way your life becomes your path for exploring and experiencing the truth.

In fact, we are all in the process of dying. Before long, the moment will arrive when we will fill a coffin. Should you really be spending your time complaining and arguing with each other? If you keep arguing about Mahayana, Theravada, right, wrong, systematic and unsystematic, then when are you going to start relying upon your fundamental mind and really grasp its essence?

Now is the time for you to be exploring the invisible realm, which is fifty percent of the whole. You should be able to use the invisible realm together with the visible realm, which is the other fifty percent of the whole. Only after you truly know both realms can you be free from the cycle of rebirth and able to live freely without ever being hindered by anything. You should be trying to achieve wisdom and trying to discover how to become a true human being, but how will you ever be able to know the invisible realm if you keep raising pointless arguments? Unless the thought of "I" dies, you will never be able to take even one step into the invisible realm.

Long ago, the patriarch Huineng* said the following about

what we call Juingong: "Who would have thought that my inherent nature is intrinsically pure? Who would have thought that this fundamental mind is inherently endowed with everything? Who would have thought that this mind is so utterly unshakable? Who would have thought that this mind receives everything and sends out everything?" This "intrinsically pure nature" is our fundamental mind. "Utterly unshakable" means that our fundamental mind is perfectly complete as it is. And the phrase "mind receives everything and sends out everything" indicates that the foundation of the entire universe is directly connected to our fundamental mind, and that everything in the universe functions together inseparably. With these few sentences, Huineng summed up the principles by which the upper realm, the middle realm, and the lower realm all function together.

If you truly know that mind is inherently and directly connected to the entire universe, you will naturally be able to take care of everything.

The Dharma Wheel has eight spokes: four spokes that represent the visible realm and four spokes that represent the invisible realm. So the Dharma Wheel and its eight spokes mean that everything in both realms works together freely and naturally. Every single thing in the universe is directly connected to the fundamental mind of human beings, and so everything functions together as one. If you truly awaken to this, you will realize that your inherent nature is intrinsically pure, that your mind is inherently endowed with everything and is complete as it is, and you will also realize that you can freely send out and take in anything through mind. All of these things will naturally become clear to you. They are inherent within you: no one else can take them away from you and no one else can give them to you.

All of this is included in what we call Juingong, the fundamental mind that each one of us is inherently endowed with, and which is directly connected to the foundation of every single thing. Thus, Juingong functions nondually with everything.

When our foundation, our Juingong, gathers together with the foundation of everything else and they all function together as one, we call this *Hanmaum*, or one mind. Hanmaum is beyond comparison with anything else and cannot be hindered by anything. Hanmaum is always working ceaselessly. Everything in the universe is directly connected to every other thing, and they all work together inseparably. Thus, without me, others would not exist, and without them, I would not exist. Juingong is not only my Juingong, which guides me during every single moment of my life, but also the Juingong of the whole, in which all things are connected to each other and are united as one. This working together of everything as one mind is called Hanmaum Juingong. We can also call Hanmaum Juingong a smelting furnace, because it melts down whatever you put into it. Hanmaum Juingong is the source of all energy, so it can also be called your inner power plant. In truth, Hanmaum Juingong is beyond words, but in order to help you grasp it, I've tried to explain it using several different descriptions.

Don't worry about whether things go well or not. Just put everything straight into the smelting furnace within you. Whatever you put into the furnace will be completely melted down and will be automatically reborn as something new. When you let go of something, don't worry about how things will turn out—this is exactly how you have to let go. After you have entrusted everything, if you start worrying about whether things will go well or not, then it's like you didn't put those things straight into the furnace. Therefore, don't worry about what will come out afterward; just put everything into the smelting furnace within you. This is the only thing you have to be concerned about. The lay practitioner Buseol* also solved the problems that confronted him by directly putting everything into his inner smelting furnace.

THE TEACHINGS OF THE LAYMAN BUSEOL

Long ago, there was a woman who was unable to speak. The year she turned nineteen, she met the monk Buseol and, upon meeting him, was suddenly able to speak for the first time in her life. As he began to leave, she clung to him, crying, "I can speak because of you! If you were to leave, there would be no life for me. If you won't marry me, I'll kill myself as soon as you go." Buseol thought to himself, "What kind of disciple of the Buddha would I be if I were to go and leave her to die? I'd disgrace the Buddha and violate the spirit of his teachings. Above all I should save her life. How could I hope to move forward and eventually achieve enlightenment if I don't face the problems that are now right in front of me?" With this view, he gave up the monastic life and married her. Such a compassionate heart!

One day, two Buddhist monks who used to practice with Buseol called on him. Because he had married, they treated him with contempt and spoke roughly to him. However, he remained calm and received them warmly. He treated them well and never argued over the things they were saying. Such deep compassion and wisdom, such profound meaning in his actions!

Nevertheless, Buseol felt that he couldn't let them leave without doing something about their mistaken views. So he filled three gourds with water and hung them in a row. Next he told the monks to each break a gourd. When each monk hit his gourd, the gourd broke and the water fell to the ground. However, when Buseol hit his gourd, the gourd shattered and the pieces fell to the ground, but the water just dangled there. It was suspended in the shape of the gourd, as if it were frozen. When the two monks saw this, they realized that they had been mistaken about the level of Buseol's spiritual practice. After some reflection, they apologized, saying, "Until now we've paid attention to only theories, without having tried to put them into practice. Further, we didn't discard the stubbornness and arrogance that arose from the idea of our having studied under so many great Seon masters. Please forgive us." Then they bowed deeply to Buseol, who looked like just another poor woodcutter. Buseol then told them that the physical body is like the gourds they broke, whereas their inherent nature is like the water dangling in the air. He taught them that our inherent nature remains just as it is and is never caught by anything. With this, the two monks became his disciples.

Like the layman Buseol, practitioners who cultivate mind shouldn't look down upon others. Regardless of whether the people you meet have wisdom or not, whether they are disabled or not, whether they are intelligent or not, whether they are a stone, a flower, or a dying tree, treat them with a smile and a broad mind. Practice diligently, and magnanimity and wisdom will well up from the bottom of your heart. You should be able to regard all of them as yourself. You behaved just like them when you didn't know any better; during a billion years of evolution, there were times when you were just like them. They are yourself. When you are able to have compassion and love for all beings, regardless of who or what they are, then you will have started on the path that leads to becoming a true human being, a person who has completely freed himself.

CULTIVATING MIND IS LIKE HIKING UP A MOUNTAIN

The process of cultivating mind can be compared to climbing up a mountain. On the way to the highest peak, imagine we come across all different kinds of luggage. Should we also carry these up the mountain? It is hard enough to get to the top carrying just our body. Should we also shoulder all of the different things we encounter? No, we should leave them behind and move on. Likewise, when we cultivate mind in everyday life, we have to let go of everything we experience. While cultivating mind, sometimes people see or hear certain things that others cannot, but this often tends to increase their pride and conceit. Also, while cultivating mind people will start to see things in sharper focus, but this can also make it easier for them to fall into distinctions between good and bad, beautiful and repulsive. These kinds of distinctions will cause every kind of desire to increase. These things will make it much harder for you to let go of your stubbornness and thoughts of "I," "me," and "mine." Yet unless you let go of these, it will be impossible to reach your destination. So you have to let go of everything and move forward. Even the luggage that we already have at the beginning of the climb—our bodies—is so heavy that we plod on under the weight of a great burden. We don't need to add any more baggage.

If you just keep letting go of everything and moving forward, you'll reach the top of the mountain. Standing on top of the mountain for the first time, you will be able to look around and see everything from a higher perspective. Seeing everything all together like this is completely different from seeing each thing by itself. Because you can see the whole, you will understand that what happens over here occurs because of what took place over there, that something which took place over there is caused by something over here. You will see that if you push down here, something rises up over there, and that if you push down over there, something responds here. Everything works together as an interconnected whole. When you can see things from this perspective, you will realize that ultimately there is no such thing as things going well or poorly; that male and female, old and young, do not exist separately; that east and west are not worlds apart; that Mahayana Buddhism and Theravada Buddhism are not separate from each other. Nor are rich and poor. Further, the person with power and the person without power do not always remain the same. You will realize all of this when you are able to see both the visible and the invisible realms together.

Furthermore, when you come down from the mountain again,

you naturally pick up what's needed from the things that were left behind, but this time you pick them up without any thought of picking them up. Because this time you picked them up free of any intention to pick them up, you are able to use them naturally, as needed, without any thought of using them.

UNWAVERING FAITH

Being able to learn about letting go and relying upon our fundamental mind is such a precious and rare opportunity. The karmic chance to learn about this is something to be deeply grateful for. Keep practicing and experimenting with letting go and entrusting until you thoroughly grasp it and can apply it in your daily life. Keep practicing diligently, and attain the ability to live your life with wisdom and compassion.

No matter how many books you read, or how many teachings you hear, and even though you can quote and speak about all those things, ultimately that won't help you a bit. Even though you study the sutras, you'll be able to understand the true meaning of the words only when you can understand the blank paper. Once you are able to truly read the words, you will be able to see all of the wisdom and truth of the entire universe contained within even a single word. So the blank paper means the wisdom of the whole, Hanmaum, and the words represent the application of this wisdom. How could you hope to become a Buddha without having experienced the wonder of both knowing and being able to use the wisdom of Hanmaum?

Let go of the idea that some thought or mental state is hindering you, and let go of even the idea that you have to practice diligently; just maintain steady, unwavering faith in your fundamental mind. Because it is inherently endowed with everything, all you have to do is believe in it. However, some of you overstrain yourself desperately trying to practice, often thinking, "Why isn't this working? I was told that if I entrusted everything, it would go well. But why isn't it working for me?" If you overstrain yourself like this, it's hard to move forward. As soon as the centipede thinks, "How can I walk so well without all these legs tripping over each other?" at that instant its legs become tangled up and unable to move. The same may be said of you. Tripped up by your own thoughts, you don't make progress in your practice, but whose fault is this? I keep teaching people about the importance of letting go of attachments, as well as how to do so, but still they don't let go of them. Even after you've let go of something, if it arises within you again, just let go of it again. However, instead of releasing it again, people tend to fret about it, thinking, "I let it go, but nothing has changed." Even the thought that letting go doesn't work is something you have to let go of and entrust to your foundation, but many people aren't doing this.

There are some people who live with the attitude, "A person can't die twice. Even if the sky is falling, I'll remain calm and deal with whatever arises, and just live in whatever situation confronts me, however bad." People like this are much better off than those who worry, and their lives turn out okay. But a person who is full of fear and clinging thinks, "Although I have let go of my problems and entrusted them to Juingong, why haven't they improved? Juingong, please help me!" This kind of behavior won't help things at all, because it's not actually letting go. If you are begging Juingong for help, then you have already begun to perceive Juingong as something separate from yourself. Your fundamental mind is yourself. Why are you treating it as if it were something apart from yourself? Stop doing this! When you already feel that things are going wrong, the way to take care of those is to entrust them to your own true nature. As Huineng said, your inherent nature is intrinsically pure! Your mind is inherently endowed with everything! Because you exist, you are already endowed with all abilities and wisdom! Because you exist, your fundamental mind perceives everything and responds accordingly! You have to experiment with and experience these truths to the point where you completely understand them and can freely and naturally apply them to whatever circumstances arise.

When we're thirsty, we just go and get a drink of water, don't we? In our daily lives, if we're in desperate need of something, our foundation naturally provides a solution. Though it may not be what we expected! Regardless of whether we are enlightened or unenlightened, this ability is inherent within all of us. We are endowed with such wonderful capabilities! We are complete just as we are! You are able to bring in and send out whatever is needed. Why do some people say, "This is too difficult, I can't do it," without even trying to experience or feel the way mind works? Instead of trying to experience this for themselves, they devote all their energy to their thoughts of "I," to their desire, and to their attachments.

For example, people these days tend to let themselves fall in love too easily and then end up crying and wailing. However, don't waste your tears over things like that. If you shed a single tear, it should be able to release a sea of compassion and wisdom, and save countless beings. If you can live your life with this kind of wisdom, then not only will you be able to obtain true freedom but also the universe will entrust the key to you. Let's talk about this next time, and use the rest of the time today for questions.

QUESTIONER 1: I am deeply grateful for your Dharma teaching and the help you've given people. I have studied Buddhism for many years. I used to study the sutras, but these days I'm reading a lot about Seon. So I understand theoretically how to become a Buddha. However, I haven't been able to put any of this into practice and experience it for myself. I think there are several reasons why I haven't been able to do this.

Ever since I was young, I've felt the need to become successful in society. However, after I started to learn about Buddhism, this goal began to seem a bit silly to me. I gradually lost interest in material things. The desires I still feel to succeed in the world have begun to seem petty. So, I've been feeling stressed for some time. Is it possible to both practice Buddhism and live well in the material world?

KUN SUNIM: I understand. As I said earlier, living your everyday life truthfully and sincerely is practicing Seon and is itself the path. Everything in the material realm ends up like the broken gourds in the story about Buseol. Our body is also like the gourd filled with water, so our fundamental mind is where we need to entrust everything. Our fundamental mind is like a smelting furnace: if you just work on entrusting it with the things that confront you, that furnace will melt them all down and turn them into something new. There's no need to worry about what will be produced afterward. Just keep letting go and entrusting until you understand for yourself the abilities of your fundamental mind. Just keep doing this unconditionally, and in all circumstances. No matter how much you want to understand this for yourself, you won't be able to make any progress until you actually start letting go.

QUESTIONER 1: My desire for wealth is not for my own benefit; it's intended for the benefit of the poor. Do I still have to discard it?

KUN SUNIM: When we're thirsty, we just drink some water without any thought of drinking. When we eat and speak, we just do it naturally. When you give something to others, just give it without any thought of giving, and move on. Just live like this. Once you give something, that's the end of it. Let go of any thoughts about having given something. Why? Because "I" doesn't exist.

A man was kissing his wife when his son entered the room and called to him, "Daddy." He let go of his wife and held up his son, saying, "Dad's here. Where have you been hiding?" While he was holding his son, the man's mother called to him from another room. He put his son down and went to his mother. He met three different people. Was he the same each time? No. He was a husband when he met his wife, a father with his son, and a son to his mother. Is any one of those identities who he truly is? No.

What people think of as "me" or "I" is always changing and never remains the same for even an instant, so it is said that "I" is empty. Everything in our life is empty; it changes every moment. Just entrust it all to your Juingong, for that is the unchanging foundation that is doing everything. Juingong is what enables everything to function together as one, but it's not some separate aspect or part. You can find it only within yourself, but it's connected to everything and functions as one with everything. So please don't think, "I did this" or "you did that." Instead, just practice comfortably, releasing even thoughts of "I let go" or "I haven't let go." Live while completely releasing such thoughts, and come to the Seon Center more often. Listen to what sunims and other practitioners say, and use that as spiritual food for your practice.

QUESTIONER 2: A serious thing has happened since the last time I had a chance to meet you. My father passed away, and we held the funeral a few days ago. I still don't know enough to call myself a Buddhist, nor am I certain about how to behave in front of a Buddhist teacher like yourself. All I am certain of is of my deep respect for you. I've read extensively in Eastern and Western philosophy, and I'm fairly confident of my understanding of what I've read. As I've listened to your Dharma talks, it's clear to me that your teachings contain the deep meanings of all those books, so I would like to ask you some questions that occurred to me after I buried my father.

First, you've said that during the years when you practiced in the mountains, you felt that graves represented the essence of the universe and so would often practice next to graves. Why did you feel that graves symbolized the essence of the universe?

Second, again today you said that when we know the invisible realm, the unseen fifty percent of reality, we can go all the way to the top of the mountain and have the ability to know the whole, to know both this realm and the other realm. If the invisible realm refers to the world after death where the spirits of the dead reside, then for people like me who are not able to see the world after death, I would be grateful if you could tell us what ghosts really are.

Third, descendants always want to find the best spot for burying their parents. Traditionally it is said that carelessly moving the grave of an ancestor, or improperly looking after it, will cause us a lot of problems. I would like to know if this is true or not.

KUN SUNIM: Sometimes graves are called "hill tops" or "places of mysteries." In Korea, we make graves round, don't we? We make round-shaped grave mounds to represent the principle of round, complete mind, which combines "before" and "after," and which also combines everything throughout heaven and earth into one. This is why we bury our parents in round graves. So if this cup were a grave, everything in the universe would be contained within it. Because everything is not two, the ones lying in the graves and the ones looking at the graves are not separate. To show this wholeness, graves are made round. So sometimes we also call the grave "profound mountain." If you think about this deeply, and see everything nondually, then this is the way to obtain the energy and wisdom of round and complete mind. Everything depends on how you think.

The living and the dead are not two; only the outer shape disappears, while its foundation remains the same, beyond both living and dying. When water freezes, it becomes ice. When the ice thaws, it becomes water again, that's all. Like the relationship between water and ice, when a person dies, he or she is called a corpse—only the label changes. Living people are not separate from those who are dead. Because all things are not two, because the minds of the past, present, and future are not separate, everything is combined together as one.

Because everything is combined together and working as one, this world we live in is sometimes described as the Buddha's monastery. Every single place contains the truth that the Buddha taught. So, long ago when someone would ask, "Where can I find the truth that the Buddha spoke of?" Seon masters would answer without using words. One Seon master drew a circle; another Seon master drew a circle and placed a dot in the center of the circle; another Seon master stepped over a corpse and then circled it three or four times, and then left; still another Seon master remained still without doing anything. How can words express the profoundness and completeness of mind?

As I said a little while ago, the person who sees the grave and the person who is in the grave are not two. The round grave signifies that the mind of "before" and the mind of "after" are gathered together. If your mind becomes bright, you will know this for yourself. If you truly know that everything is not two, you will attain and be able to use the energy and wisdom of everything working together as one. So please thoroughly explore the principle of non-duality while entrusting everything to your Juingong.

What was your other question?

QUESTIONER 2: It's often believed that if we do something improperly in the process of moving an ancestor's body or taking care of a grave, this will give rise to a lot of problems in our lives. Is this true?

KUN SUNIM: Ah, that was it. If you cultivate your mind, you don't need to worry about that. Cultivating mind means completely letting go of everything—including all doctrines such as Mahayana, Theravada, and everything else—and exploring the truth that everything works as one. So if you are really cultivating mind, how could the way you take care of the graves of your ancestors be the cause of good or bad things? Mind has no form. Do you understand? So even if you were to put a thousand spirits or consciousnesses into your mind, or were to take them out of your mind, there would be no problem, because they're not something separate from yourself. In fact, as you're searching for a place to bury your parents, if you have a good feeling about a certain place, then that's the proper place for burying them. This practice encompasses and includes all scientific fields such as geology, astronomy, medicine, and astrophysics. In other words, you are learning how to live according to the rhythms of the truth and how to freely use that energy. So please don't let yourself be chained by thoughts like that.

As you know from experience, if you rely on good luck charms or believe in superstitions, you can't do even the smallest task without worrying. However, when you discard such superstitious ideas, your life will have fewer troubles, and things will actually turn out even better for you than before. Just to earn a living you have to endure so many bothersome things; also, so many people live without having any idea of where they came from, where they are going, or how to live as a true person. In these circumstances, isn't it kind of sad to spend your life feeling additional anxiety because of superstitions? Let go of everything! Don't worry about anything. Don't cling to anything. If you live while entrusting all things to your foundation, everything will be all right.

QUESTIONER 3: I have studied Buddhism on my own and have had some questions for a while, but I didn't know who to ask. Anyway, I came to the Hanmaum Seon Center for the first time today and would like to ask you about those things.

It seems like the world is flooded by evil and is becoming more corrupt as time goes by. Also, the population seems to be increasing in proportion to the growing corruption of the world. However, in Buddhism we are told that it is hard to be born as a human being, because one must first accumulate a lot of virtue in order to receive a human body. Why does the population keep increasing when it's said that it is very difficult to be reborn as a human being?

Also, in other religions it is said that God created the world, but how does Buddhism explain the beginning of the world? According to the Buddhist texts I've read, mind caused the existence of this world. In Buddhism we are told that each and every being has Buddha-nature, and the inherent nature of human beings is clean and pure. I would like to know how this clean and pure mind was able to move in the beginning, and how it created everything in the universe?

KUN SUNIM: Everything in the universe is made of earth, water, fire, and air. Your body is also a combination of earth, water, fire, and air. The lives within your body are also made of these four elements. Furthermore, we live by eating earth, water, fire, and air from outside of our body, don't we? Our bodies rely upon these elements because our bodies arose from them. This cup in my hand also came into being because earth, water, fire, and air combined together. All matter is formed by the combination of these elements. When the four elements were separate, they were incapable of producing life. However, when they combined together, they produced a life form, and from this, all other beings began to develop.

In passing through myriads of eons, there were times when we did good things and times when we did bad things. There were times when we behaved foolishly and times when we behaved wisely. As we lived like this, we developed the ability to raise One Thought,* to connect to our foundation and communicate with everything throughout the universe, and through that evolutionary power we've developed to the level of human beings. Because of the evolutionary power that arises from all our accumulated experiences, we humans are called the highest animal. Let's look at the example of the rabbit. Originally, a rabbit's legs were all the same length. But when they ran up hills, they couldn't run very fast because their legs were the same length, and they were easily caught and eaten. After many such experiences, they raised a thought that "My front legs need to be a little shorter. I wish my front legs weren't so long." Afterward, they were born with shorter front legs.

Hmm, many of you don't seem to understand... Let's look at the example of prenatal education. There was a husband and wife who were both good-looking, but this was because they'd both had plastic surgery. When they gave birth to a son, he wasn't that attractive, because he resembled his parents' original appearances.

So people would say, "How did such good-looking parents give birth to such a homely baby?" However, when the wife was pregnant with their second child, someone told them, "Don't think of your original appearances. Instead, think of your grandfather, who was very handsome. While thinking of his face and strong body, describe that to your unborn child. Visualize your child having that appearance." This time they had a good-looking baby who resembled his great-grandfather.

This is how mind works. Mind has neither hands nor feet nor body. Yet it can reach even an unborn child. When you draw a good-looking face with your mind, your child will be good-looking. This is possible because at the level of our eternal foundation, the mind of the unborn child and the mind of its parents are not separate from each other. Whether we are old or young, this is not the only life we will live. Don't think that there is no next life. Even though leaves fall from a tree in the autumn, in the spring, they will reappear. I hope that you will all use the evolutionary ability of mind to draw a good shape for your next life.

The well-being of the nation also depends upon how we use our minds. The president and congressmen are elected when the majority of votes are cast for them. In the same way, if the minds of many people lean toward evil, this evil force can cause all kinds of disasters and disturbances. Everything depends upon mind! Like-wise, when you use mind wisely, your invisible foundation knows that thought and causes it to manifest into this world, so everything will go well.

When the circumstances are ripe, difficult problems occur in this world on a regular cycle; sometimes it's every five hundred years, sometimes it's every thousand years, and sometimes it's every one hundred thousand years. We have wealth and technology unmatched in human experience, but these things often end up causing a lot of problems because the level of our mind is too low to receive and digest them. Thus we lose many of the benefits of these technological and material developments. Technology has developed so rapidly, but we have not been able to properly handle those changes because the development of our mind has not kept pace. Think about a bowl. If the bowl is too small, it can't hold very much, and anything more than that overflows and causes a mess.

This is the origin of the problem. Therefore, we have to start by making our minds broader and deeper. To do this, firmly let go of all thoughts such as "Mahayana Buddhism," "Theravada Buddhism," "Things are going well," "Things are going badly," or "I am the best."

Ask about this problem again next time. Even when you ask questions, ask questions without any thought of asking. Then your questions will become fertilizer for everyone's practice.

QUESTIONER 4: After reading one of your books, I came here today for the first time to listen to your Dharma talk. My son was born last May. I was so happy then, but from the time he was about a month old, he's been so sick that he seems to hang between life and death. We went to many different hospitals before he was eventually diagnosed with cerebral palsy. I feel that this disease must be the karmic result of my own wrongdoings. How can I repay my debts and save my child? I am completely lost.

KUN SUNIM: I've used this example before: gold is kept with gold, iron with iron, silver with silver, and apples with apples. Like this, people with similar karma gather together. The past causes are directly connected to the present effects. The person who sees the suffering and the person who is suffering both gather together and suffer because of the similar causes they each created in the past. Without any conscious awareness of what's going on, they are naturally drawn together because of their similar karma. Like the noise from two empty cans hitting together, each of you has contributed to that situation, so now both of you are experiencing that hardship together. So how can we resolve problems caused by our past behaviors?

Entrust each and every thing to your fundamental place, to Juingong. You should know that the entire universe is directly connected to the fundamental mind of each person. So believe in your foundation and entrust everything to it. Because your child's disease came from the foundation as karmic retribution, you should release it to the place it came out from, the foundation. Entrust your son's illness to Juingong, knowing that this disease arose from Juingong, so it's Juingong that can cure it. Then, like water changing into vapor, everything will change. The karma that has caused your suffering will completely disappear. When you fall down, you are the one who has to pick yourself up. There is no one else who brings you suffering, and there is no one else who takes it away. You are the one who made it, so you are also the one who can solve it.

You have to return your problem to the place it came from. Then the karmic consciousnesses within you that are causing that problem will be reborn as Bodhisattvas. When this happens, all of the karma that causes you to be mistreated, unjustly accused, and so forth, will all vanish. Then all of the beings within your son's body and brain will become active and supply and circulate energy throughout his body. So his condition will improve. This is not just some theory. However, the only way to know this truth is through doing and trying. You have to make an effort to apply this for yourself; then you'll experience it. When you have experienced this, your faith and sincerity deepen, and you'll know, "Ah, this is it! Every single thing, whether small or big, all comes from myself." Because you came into this world, everything in your life came into existence. Even things like *hwadus,** phrases meant to spark enlightenment, exist only because you exist. You're the source of everything in your life, so you're the one who is capable of taking care of it all.

Some people complain that things at the temple aren't very well organized, or they argue about whether what we teach here is Theravada Buddhism or Mahayana Buddhism. Furthermore, some also speak ill of sunims. However, let's think about sunims. Even though they occasionally make mistakes, they've left behind their parents and siblings, and haven't married. On the path to the truth, they walk alone, wearing the gray clothes of someone determined to realize the middle way. Laypeople grow their hair long and style it, but sunims have shaved off their hair. At some point they decided to throw away everything and determined to cultivate mind to the exclusion of all else, and in doing so, have already made great strides. So should you really be criticizing or finding fault with them?

Regardless of their mistakes, you shouldn't behave like that if you are someone who is determined to cultivate mind. Laypeople who achieved enlightenment, such as Buseol and Vimalakirti,* never said a word criticizing sunims. They just helped sunims to awaken. However, some of you speak ill of sunims, saying, "Look at the examples set by Buseol and Vimalakirti. Even though they didn't shave their hair, they practiced so diligently. These sunims today are worthless." I hope that you will discard this kind of discriminatory mind. When you see even the robes that sunims wear, have a humble and respectful mind toward them. When you see that sunims have no spouse or children, don't you feel humbled by what they go through?

Why don't you feel any pity for sunims? In the case of laypeople, a man and a woman share their life together and take care of each other. They help each other with meals, worry about each other's clothing when the weather is bad, keep each other warm at night, and get a glass of water when the other is thirsty. However, sunims are all alone in the world. No one else looks after them when they are hungry or cold. If you were in their situation, wouldn't you feel some compassion for yourself? Even though you have a lot of hardships in your life, doesn't the life of a sunim seem even harder? So, shouldn't you have some sympathy for them? Even though sunims may not have awakened, even though they ignore their responsibilities, behave badly, or even fight and argue, if you think a bit more about their lives, you'd feel much more compassion for them.

Suppose your brother or sister shaved his or her hair and left home to become a sunim. If you saw them making such efforts to become an awakened person, wouldn't you feel grateful to them? If you thought of yourself experiencing the same hardships as the sunims you see, you could never speak ill of them. If you deeply felt their situation, your heart would reach out for them as if they were your own children, parents, or siblings. I feel so glad when I see the gray clothes that sunims wear. Regardless of whether they are a good sunim or not, regardless of whether they are doing well or not, I feel grateful when I see them wearing these gray clothes.

In the Korean flag, there is a circle in the center that is divided into heaven and earth, and in each corner of the flag is a set of three, four, five, or six lines. The flag was drawn like that to indicate that everything in the universe is one interconnected whole.

Summed up, it means that the universe's foundation is the foundation of human beings, and that human beings' foundation is the foundation of the universe.

So if you are determined to rely upon and discover your fundamental mind, then no matter how worthless a person you meet, you should regard that person as yourself, thinking, "That's what I was like once, when I was ignorant, when I was still learning how to become a human being." If you are able to practice like this, your son will completely recover.

I saw some cases like this when I was visiting the U.S., in San Jose and New York. There was a baby who suffered from a brain disorder similar to your son's. He couldn't move his body and was almost in a coma. However, his parents and his uncle were extremely sincere in entrusting everything to Juingong. When they brought him here last time, although he hadn't completely recovered physically, I saw that he had become an affectionate and inquisitive boy. Who helped him to become like that? Good results were able to occur because his family members were also practicing very sincerely, and this combined with the sunims' minds. Generally speaking, even though a sunim raises good thoughts for someone, that person also has to be practicing diligently in order for the connection to be made between them.

If your mind is bright, you can help others to live brightly. If only one person in a family awakens to this principle of one mind, that person becomes a light of wisdom for the rest of their family. If you brighten your mind, then that light shines upon others and brightens their lives. So the people around you feel at ease, and they become more harmonious and live their lives well. It is not enough to understand this principle intellectually. You have to put it into practice and experience it for yourself by believing in your Juingong and entrusting it with everything.

THE STORY OF THE PRECIOUS LOTUS BUDDHA

If there are no other questions, I would like to continue with a topic I mentioned a while ago. When we observe this phenomenal realm in which we live, sometimes disease, suffering, disasters, wars, and poverty seem suddenly to occur everywhere, and at other times they just disappear. Do you know why? It's because this phenomenal world that we live in is always connected to and interacts with the Dharma realm.

Let me tell you an old story. Listen carefully, and don't think of this as just a story. Once upon a time, there was a brother and sister who were born a year apart, to a very poor family. When the children were three and two years old, both their parents died in the same year, and the children became orphans, wandering from place to place. One day a sunim found them, and touched by their pitiful condition, he arranged for a temple to take care of them. The boy was sent to the monk's hall, and the girl was sent to the nun's hall, and there they grew up.

One night, when the girl was eighteen years old, a lady who looked exactly like her suddenly appeared in a dream, and said, "Listen carefully. One hundred thousand years ago, a group of evil spirits caused great confusion in the heavenly realm that I come from. If such confusion is allowed to continue in that heavenly realm, evil influences will spread out everywhere, and this world of yours will also fall into chaos. Diseases and disasters will reign, and the world will verge upon extinction. At that time, we produced a great star called the Precious Lotus Buddha. This was able to stop the spread of evil influences in the heavenly realm, and in so doing it also saved this world from destruction. From now on you need to diligently cultivate mind so that you will be able to bring back the Precious Lotus Buddha. For there are calamities due to return in five hundred years, and without regenerating the Precious Lotus Buddha they cannot be avoided. Keep practicing diligently. Then when the difficult times come, you will be able to make the Precious Lotus Buddha reappear.

"You will know these calamities have returned when it rains so continuously that people can no longer see the earth, when the wind blows so strongly that it shakes heaven and earth, when the fog and clouds are so thick that people can't see the sun or the moon. People will lose their leader and just wander about, or they will behave as if they have no leader, or their leader himself will ignore the people. Surviving will be very difficult for everyone. Furthermore, the minds of the people and other living beings will become so severely confused and disturbed that parents won't look after their children, and children won't take care of their parents, while diseases, disasters, and wars will prevail all over the world.

"Thus you must practice now, so that when difficult times come, you will be able to cause the great star to reappear. If you can combine your mind with the great star, the Precious Lotus Buddha, it will become bright once again. When the star reappears, its light will protect the entire world. However, if you are unable to do this, the world may be completely destroyed. Therefore, you must practice very diligently and be able to do what I have told you."

Although the lady said that those things were going to happen in five hundred years, those five hundred years can be only an instant. For people who are practicing, five hundred years in the future or five hundred years in the past are only an instant. However, for people who don't practice, five hundred years lasts for five hundred years.

In the dream, the lady continued, "If you can bring back the great light and save the heavenly realm, you will also bring peace back to this world. The calamities of this world will gradually lessen, life will flourish again, and all will be at peace."

Upon hearing this, the sister asked, "After regenerating the Precious Lotus Buddha, how do we get rid of the evil?" The lady answered, "It is not something to be gotten rid of. Listen carefully, and I will explain: Mara, the King of Evil, creates a large number of evil spirits, places them under his command, and then uses them to invade the heavenly realm. If the heavenly realm is plunged into chaos, the human world also falls into chaos. However, if the heavenly realm is peaceful, the human world also becomes peaceful. The number of those evil spirits grows larger and larger because their evil minds bring forth even more evil. And that new evil again brings forth more evil, and so on. However, when the great star reappears, it embraces everything and shines upon all things. Once this happens, those evil spirits weaken and melt away. They just vanish; they are not actual physical beings. When the light embraces them, their evil minds change to good and they all become one. Helping them change like this is true compassion."

It's possible for that evil to just vanish because it's like a shadow, it's not something with a true existence.

The lady in the dream continued, "When people's minds become confused, and evil tendencies increase, these disasters can happen again. They could happen every thousand years or every billion years. The entire world could fall into chaos and destruction, or it could rise again afterward. It could be destroyed by fires and floods, or these things could be completely prevented. There is only one thing that can take care of all these problems—mind."

If you completely understand how mind works and are able to combine your mind with others' minds, and if you are able to deepen your wisdom and continue to practice, then you can combine your mind with even the great stars of the heavenly realm. When you can do this, the heavenly realm becomes peaceful and comfortable, and in turn this world also becomes peaceful and comfortable. When confusion occurs in the heavenly realm, it is as if that confusion were happening on the roof of our own house. This confusion in the heavenly realm causes all kinds of problems in our realm—the winds blow and dust storms arise, the land goes down and the water rises up, and people become confused and stop behaving like human beings. This could be called the final, degenerate age, or the end of the world.

PUT EVERYTHING INTO THE SMELTING FURNACE
WITHIN YOU

If you are determined to cultivate your mind, don't let yourself fall into discriminatory thoughts; you don't need to make discriminations such as "Mahayana Buddhism" or "Theravada Buddhism," "systematic" or "unsystematic." Even those thoughts are a kind of delusion, so don't let yourself be distracted by them. The only thing you need to do is to put every single thing into your inner furnace, into Juingong. Whether things go well or badly is balanced upon a single thought. They can change in less than an instant. So when things turn out well, let go of them with gratitude. And when things aren't going well, let go of them, knowing, "Juingong is taking care of things, so they will turn out for the best." Even when you suffer from illness, you should entrust it, thinking, "Only Juingong can cure my illness." Even if you suffer from poverty, you should entrust it with the thought that "only Juingong can help me to be better off." If you can do this, it will be possible to help all of the beings within your body to evolve, and you will have wisdom and the capacity to live freely and go forward with a smile.

Don't concern yourself with what other people say about the principle of one mind. Let go when you know the reason for something, and let go when you don't know the reason, and just go forward without getting caught up in things like this. Our life is like a drifting cloud that lasts only for a moment. Everything changes its shape every moment, and this changing and flowing is truth itself.

Although a bottle full of water breaks, that water still exists, doesn't it? It just changes its shape and flows naturally. All things flow like this, just as they are. You wouldn't be able to live otherwise. You should always be grateful for the four elements: earth, water, fire, and air. We should feel grateful for every single thing in the world. Every single thing is our teacher.

It seems there are no more questions today. Next time we meet, if you have a question about something, be sure to ask me. Although I've taught you to let go of everything, don't think that this means that you shouldn't ask questions. There is an old saying that even when you cross a stone bridge, you should still test it before crossing. Although you may think you already know the answer, you can still ask the question again, both to check your understanding and for the sake of other people who might not know. Let go of all your ideas and thoughts about asking questions and just do it.

Although we cannot see the electricity coming and going, the light still turns on. Even though you can see the wiring, you cannot see the electricity moving. Likewise, you cannot see the mind of human beings coming and going. Thoroughly understand how this unseen mind works, and live wisely. I hope that you will learn to apply your compassion through both the visible and invisible realms, and I also hope that you will put into practice and experience for yourself what you have learned today. Let's stop here for today.

Let Go and Observe

Once again, we are meeting here together as fellow practitioners. Today I'd like to talk about the fact that we have to put our understanding into practice and apply it to all parts of our daily life. I'd like to talk about this, because before trying to become a Buddha, a Bodhisattva, or the embodiment of the Dharma, we must first learn to become true human beings.

When our every thought is returned to and arises from the fundamental place, this is called the essence of meditation. If you attain the essence of meditation, you will also be able to uphold the essence of the precepts. It is not just monastics who uphold the essence of the precepts. As I often tell you: treat others kindly, without making distinctions. See their pain as your pain, and see them as your own children, parents, and siblings. Do not see even a plant as something separate from yourself. In so doing, you will attain wisdom and become free from attachment. Then everyone else will become free together with you. There is no person who is inherently evil. Rather, all evil acts are the result of ignorance. People commit bad actions because of ignorance, and then, in various ways, they suffer the consequences of what they have made.

As I once said, the past doesn't exist because it exists within the present, and the future doesn't exist because it hasn't come yet. Let's take the analogy of a watermelon. Where is the seed that was planted and grew into the watermelon? That seed now exists within the watermelon; you won't find it somewhere else. If you have trouble understanding this analogy, then you may not yet perceive your own root. Just as a tree cannot see its own root, you may be unaware of your own root. It's hard to find, because unlike a tree's root, a human being's root isn't a material thing that you can see with your eyes. Why do we struggle, searching outwardly for the past seed, our Buddha-nature, when that seed is always within us?

In order to discover your Buddha-nature, stop clinging to intellectual knowledge or to the idea that things have to be done in a certain way. And sitting in meditation all day long won't help. Eternal truth exists in every place and functions without ceasing. You should thoroughly understand that everything originates and ends at the same place, your foundation. Everything you encounter is done by that place. Everything you do is done by that place. You must absolutely know this. Because you exist, everything in your world exists, and all the lives within your body exist.

Once the Bodhisattva Manjusri* asked the lay practitioner Vimalakirti, "What kind of karma brought about your illness, and how can it be cured?" Vimalakirti replied, "When all the lives in my body are cured, won't I also be cured?" This means that when you experience and apply these teachings for yourself, through your own body, wisdom arises spontaneously. Don't hear this as a theory; you have to grasp the meaning behind it. Manjusri then asked, "Why is this room empty, why is there no one to help you?" Vimalakirti answered, "Every Buddha realm is also empty, and all heretics and demons are helping me."

Then why is it said that things are neither empty nor existing? Because everything changes moment by moment, there is no particular identity that you can claim to be your true identity. Thus, it is said that all is empty. In other words, all things are empty because although they have an existence, they are all constantly changing. Also, all beings in both the visible and invisible realms live together, sharing and learning from each other, without distinguishing between even Buddhas and unenlightened beings. That is why Vimalakirti said that all heretics and demons were helping him.

For example, there is a saying, "Water and mountains are not separate, so water exists as water, and the mountains exist as mountains." All things have their own role to perform, but they all function as one. Although they function together as one, they also exist separately. Each has a different appearance, different experiences, and is at a different place in its life. Things that belong in cups are put in cups, things that belong on plates are put on plates, and things that belong in bowls are put in bowls. Each container is used naturally, according to its purpose. If you do not understand this simple principle, everything will seem complicated. The truth that applies to one thing applies to all other things. There is nothing that exists apart from everything else.

People use the names of various Bodhisattvas to describe the mind of Buddha, but it is they themselves who play the roles of Bodhisattvas and the roles of the transformation bodies of Buddha. When you look at many Dharma halls, you can see that people have placed Manjusri on one side of the Buddha and the Bodhisattva Samantabhadra on the other side. However, in the way that the sprout, the watermelon, and the seed are not separate, so too Buddha-nature, Manjusri, and Samantabhadra are also not separate. Buddha-nature is the Buddha that exists before any thoughts arise. When a thought arises from our foundation, it becomes Manjusri, the embodiment of the Dharma. And when that thought manifests outwardly, it becomes Samantabhadra, the embodiment of transformation. To say it another way, when you are calm, you are in the state before thoughts arise. When you generate a thought through your foundation, you become an embodiment of the Dharma, and when you act upon that thought, you are the embodiment of transformation.

For example, if you trip and fall, you immediately get up and dust yourself off. In doing this, you yourself become the embodiment of Samantabhadra. If you help someone else to get up, you also become the embodiment of Samantabhadra. And if you help someone through mind, through the unseen realm, you again become Samantabhadra. Only your role in relation to others changes; when you are with your parents, you become a child; when you are with your own children, you become a parent.

You have to see the underlying essence. Even if you read a sutra, you must be able to see the essence that underlies it. Then you'll be able to truly read it. And when you can put even one phrase into practice in your daily life, you can become a true human being and a true disciple of the Buddha. As I said before, when you talk to your children, speak gently, and treat them with a nondualistic mind. This simple action is the first step on the path to becoming a Bodhisattva.

One day, Manjusri asked, "Why is it said that everything is empty?"

Vimalakirti replied, "It is because everything is inherently empty."

Manjusri asked, "How can emptiness, which is inherently empty, be experienced?"

Vimalakirti replied that Manjusri would be able to experience emptiness if he did not distinguish between "empty" and "not empty."

Manjusri responded, "Then where can I find emptiness?"

"Emptiness can be found within the sixty-two views."

"Where can I find the sixty-two views?"

"Within the enlightenment of the Buddha."

Finally, Manjusri asked, "Where is the enlightenment of the Buddha?"

Vimalakirti replied, "Within the minds of sentient beings."

In other words, the whole world can be found within Hanmaum. Consequently, all the things that you are looking for are within your one mind.

Remember what I've said: "Because you existed, because tiny plants and bugs existed, I was able to know, feel, and experience the truth. Thus, everyone is my friend, my fellow practitioner, and my teacher." All of you experience difficult things in your lives such as worries, poverty, and illness. Taking good care of your children is very difficult, as is taking care of yourself. There are so many difficult things that you have to do. However, this principle leads to great benefit and development. If you understand even a little bit of this profound principle, and gradually apply it in your everyday life, you will have composure in your life and will feel peaceful and free.

When I see what confronts people, both from within and without, it seems like there are lots of problems that overwhelm them. There are problems related to genetics, to karma, and to spirit possession, as well as everyday problems such as money and family conflicts. How can these things be resolved? You should entrust everything you encounter to your foundation. That's the only place that can truly solve your problems. Firmly entrust everything that arises to the fundamental self, Juingong, and keep watching. This isn't praying to something outside yourself for a certain outcome or thing. When you entrust everything with firm faith, what's the result? Karma dissolves, the habits of eons melt away, and you discover your true self. If you input everything you encounter into your foundation, it will all be taken care of automatically.

For example, when someone is troubled by a mental disease, some people may hastily conclude that a spirit has taken possession of that person's mind. If you fully believe that only your inner true self, Juingong, can lead you, then how could anything else enter you? Even if some ghost is already within you, you must let go of the thought that it is inside you. If you cannot let go of that thought, how can that spirit leave you? Also, why do you think that the spirit or other people are different from you? Even if a spirit enters you, it's still like putting one drop of water into a bowl of water. I've said this many times, but people spend years suffering and have many difficulties in life because they don't let go of their own fixed ideas.

Mind has no limitations. Even if a spirit enters someone and tries to take over, we should understand that all beings are still contained within one mind, within Hanmaum. Why would we consider that spirit's mind to be separate from our own mind? We can grasp this principle only when we no longer view anything as being separate from ourselves. Even if ten spirits enter someone, that person should firmly rely on Juingong, saying within himself or herself, "All things are one, so regardless of what happens, it's still my Juingong that's in charge of them. My Juingong is the one that can correctly guide this body!" This single thought of relying on Juingong is more important than performing a hundred ceremonies.

It's the lack of wisdom that causes people to suffer. Even with money, you have to know how to handle it wisely. In fact, learning to use your money wisely is even more important than knowing how to earn it. If you don't use it wisely, your life will be a whirlwind of confusion and pain.

You've never heard me tell anyone that their hardships or poverty are due to their past misdeeds, have you? This is because the difficulties people have in their lives are caused by their levels of thought. The reason you're suffering now isn't because of some bad karma that you created in the past. You're suffering because you don't know the truth. Remind yourself, "Even if ten spirits are living within me, I am still the master of my life and can take care of everything." But don't just leave this as words. You have to keep sincerely trusting that Juingong, the master within, can take care of all these situations, ensuring that they will turn out for the best. Most people can't even begin to imagine the power of their fundamental mind, their true nature. Because mind has no limitations and is not separate from anything, mind can go and explore anywhere, even beyond the earth and universe.

It is not because the mountain is too high that mind cannot pass over it, and it is not because water is too deep that mind cannot cross over it. It is not because the silver mountains and iron walls are too thick that mind does not penetrate them. It's the way you're using your mind that limits and blocks you. All directions are wide open. Let all minds now take the middle path. Let all minds learn to use both the visible and invisible realms.

I have often mentioned the five subtle powers: the power to know past and future lives, the power to know the minds of others, the power to hear anything, the power to go anywhere, and the power to see anything. However, there is nothing extraordinary about these abilities because each of you has them within yourself— you just don't recognize them. Also, there are many machines these days that function like those powers, such as radios, airplanes, computers, and telescopes.

One example of these types of machines is radar systems. There are many different components, each of which is performing its own role, while working as part of the whole. The five subtle powers are also like this. If *nujin** (the state where one is free of all the things that cause suffering) is the whole radar system, then the five subtle powers are like the different machines that are attached to the system. However, unlike a machine, the vast and profound abilities of a human being function automatically, according to the thoughts we give rise to.

All of these are able to function because of this pillar of mind that we all have. Although it doesn't move, it enables everything to manifest and function. Thus, how things go depends upon our thoughts. For example, a broad and generous mind is like a lubricant: it allows everything to move smoothly. Whereas a narrow mind is like rust: it inhibits movement and prevents the system from functioning well.

Thus, it's possible for the things in your life to go smoothly and freely, but for this to happen you have to put everything you encounter into your foundation. Yet, when I say, "Entrust everything to your own foundation," people keep asking me why and how, without making an effort to try and do this.

Even when things go well, you should still let go of all of those to your fundamental mind, with gratitude. If things aren't going the way you intended, you should entrust those matters to your fundamental mind with the thought, "It is you, Juingong, who makes things turn out well, and it is also you who causes things to not go the way I want. You're the one that can take care of everything." Entrust all the situations in your life like this. Once something is input, it functions automatically according to how you've input it.

All of the bad things, the good things, the foolish things, and the intelligent things you've done are automatically input, and will eventually return to you. Yet still some people grumble that this principle is too hard to understand. The things that arise from inside your mind or that come to you from outside are all automatically recorded within you, according to how you react to them. All of us are living like this at this very moment. Don't become someone who is always dependent upon others. Instead, practice and experience this principle for yourself, and live with freedom and dignity.

If you thoroughly input what I'm telling you, it will arise later when you need it. However, I often feel that my words just are bouncing off and coming back to me. This is really frustrating. We use mind in such an infinite variety of ways that it is said that not even one fixed thing exists, or that everything is empty. Every single movement you make and everything you see changes continuously, just like mind. Thus, all Buddhas have always said that everything is empty. There are several expressions such as "does not exist," "empty," "void," and others, but you should understand that they all have the same meaning.

Well, I've used a lot of examples, but the key point is that you need to view things positively, and input them positively. Even though you have a bad dream, don't get caught up in worries that something awful will happen. If you keep inputting all of the negative possibilities, nothing will turn out well for you. No matter whether the sky collapses or the earth is torn to pieces, simply let go of everything with firm determination. Even though death is staring you in the face, do not worry about it—let go of both life and death.

Bodhisattvas don't even cling to life or death, so how could they be caught by anything else? Yet unenlightened beings are so attached to life and death. They view living and dying through the lens of desire and aversion. Demons and heretics indulge in such narrow views, but Bodhisattvas are never swayed by those ideas. Let go of both the thoughts "I am going to die" and "I don't want to die." Even if you are on the verge of dying right now, it's not a big deal. You can't die twice. Bodhisattvas see both sides of life and death contained within everything. Thus, they don't try to avoid one aspect or the other. This is why it's said, "Nothing is clung to, so there's nothing to let go of."

I would also like to say something about cause and effect. Simply speaking, the only thing you have to worry about is just inputting things wisely. For instance, confidently raise the thought, "True self, when the time comes, let me die without pain. You're the only one that can do this." When you do this, that thought is input into your foundation. You are perfectly free to use this ability, but it is your stubborn, fixed ideas that prevent you from seeing your genuine self and using this ability. Sometimes it feels like I've been talking to a wall. People don't bother to learn to practice correctly, and then come and ask me things like, "Which date will be auspicious to move into a new house?" When they say things like this, my eyes fill with tears, and I ask myself, "After all these years, does no one understand?" Please, make greater efforts to break through the iron wall, to break through your own fixed ideas. Inputting is really very simple.

The five subtle powers are related to types of energy, such as magnetic energy, light energy, and communication ability, which are infinite and latent within each of us. For example, there is a big difference between a doctor who treats a patient while understanding this truth and a doctor who doesn't know anything about it. If the cause of a disease came from within, the doctor should be able to help the patient cure himself from inside. If the disease was caused by outside factors, the doctor should find them and try to cure the patient using all of his combined knowledge. For example, in the case of a person with schizophrenia, constantly remind the patient that it's his own foundation, Juingong, that can cure him. Teach him to keep inputting this truth. This way of treating such a patient is much better than any other kind of treatment.

Mind has no hindrance. The same energy that exists outside our bodies also exists inside our bodies, and all the four elements—earth, water, fire, and air—function together inside our body just as they function outside of it. Regardless of whether something is big or small, they all function the same. If you must go someplace a thousand miles away, you can go there without moving your body. We all carry such ability within ourselves.

Because the world today is changing so much faster than in the past, if you live without brightening your mind, everything will be confusing and you'll be left behind. You should think deeply about this. If the bus has already left, it doesn't matter how long you wait.

The bus is gone. Thus what you should do is take every single thing as it confronts you and entrust it to your inherent nature. Do this so that it becomes as natural as eating food when you're hungry, as natural as going to the toilet when you have to relieve yourself, and as natural as drinking water when you're thirsty. In other words, entrust everything to your foundation as it comes to you and watch what happens. If you observe carefully, you will see the manifestation of what was input. If you put something in, a response comes out. This is experimenting and experiencing.

When I explain how to practice in detail like this, it sounds easy, so many people think that the process of learning is very simple and as a result they don't try to practice wholeheartedly. Don't let this remain mere intellectual understanding. I want you, with a sincere heart and firm belief, to regard everything as being part of yourself, to feel other's pain as your own pain, and to try to apply what you understand. Show respect and love to your parents, be loyal to your country, keep your promises, and don't drink to excess. If you often drink too much, you'll lose the brightness of your mind. This is bad for you, of course, but it's also very harmful to others.

The reason you are told not to kill is because the life of every being in the world is the same as your life, and their pain is your pain. If you're truly aware of this, you cannot treat other beings cruelly. However, if your parents or children have been sick, and eating a chicken would help them, then let's say you buy a chicken and thereby indirectly kill it. While you are doing that, entrust the whole action to your Juingong, wholeheartedly trusting that you and the chicken are not separate. Then, even though it can be

---

called killing, it's no longer truly killing. Because you have combined the chicken's mind as one with your mind, and input this togetherness into your foundation, only its body falls away. All you've done is remove its ignorance. Even so, do not recklessly kill or eat anything you like. Not every killing can be justified. Cruel, deliberate killing is much worse.

Let me tell you a story. Long ago, there was a sunim who lived with his teacher in a small, run-down temple deep in the mountains. One day, the teacher became very ill. However, being so poor and so isolated, the sunim didn't have any healthy food to help his teacher recover, so he caught hundreds of earthworms and boiled them to make a broth for his teacher. While cooking the earthworms, the sunim thought, "If these can help my teacher recover, I don't care what happens to me or what kind of birth I might have in my next life." Eventually, the teacher recovered after eating all of the earthworm broth. He asked his disciple where he had obtained the delicious "medicine." So the sunim answered his teacher, "Oh, I made it from some leaves I picked off a tree in the deep forest." Also, thanks to that sunim, those earthworms were able to evolve to a higher level when they became one with the teacher.

Just living gently and passively is not what the Buddha taught. You have to also be able to wisely overcome the difficulties in your life. This is also a part of your spiritual practice. If you don't know how to handle things, or are too dependent, this causes difficulties for the people around you, as well as for yourself. Input the desire that you don't want to be like that into your Juingong, then, the consciousness of each cell within your body will become firmly integrated with that thought. If you're diligent about this, every-thing that arises from the inside or the outside will be led by the thoughts you give rise to.

You don't have to sit in meditation all day. Please keep on work-ing hard at whatever your job is, and try to spend a half-hour or so observing your mind after the day's work or whenever you have some spare time. While watching, entrust everything to your inherent self and give rise to the thought, "Juingong! Because you exist, I came into being, and so I'm thinking of you. And because you are the only one who has the ability to take care of all things, I entrust them all to you. Unlike my present awareness, you know everything because you have been here through hundreds of mil-lions of years of evolution and creation. So please reveal your will to me." You can call your foundation, "my beloved," "Juingong," or "my inner self"; the name isn't important. What is important is entrusting everything to Juingong and then applying what you experience. You need to challenge yourself to do this. However, entrusting everything to your foundation is not begging or praying for the things you want. Those things are just reflections of your own fixed ideas.

In all the things that come up in your life, practice relying upon your fundamental mind. Try to do this sincerely and with firm faith. We are all in the same boat, so even a single ball of rice will benefit everyone. In fact, if we can all live together harmoniously, that single ball of rice will be more than enough to feed all of the beings in the universe. You really need to know this for yourself.

I'll end my talk here.

Walking without a Trace

It's getting cold these days, so I hope that you and your families will all be healthy this winter. If you fully awaken to this fundamental mind and how it works, happiness will always find your family. The potential of this practice is just so vast and incredible that words can't even begin to approach it. Keep practicing and experiencing with everything. Don't miss anything, from the trivial to the most significant.

Coming to the temple isn't enough. You won't make any real progress until you start getting rid of "I" and "me." If you discard just this illusion of "I," all difficulties will subside. Your worries will disappear. But if you don't discard these persistent thoughts of "I did this" or "I must live," which are based on your concepts of the material world, you cannot die. This does not mean the death of the body. Since everything continuously flows and works together and nothing remains stationary or unchanging, "dying" means letting yourself go within that.

When a stream meets a boulder, look at how the water behaves: it flows around it and continues onward. When there's a lot of rain, the raindrops gather together and eventually flow into the ocean. Similarly, no matter what kinds of problems you face, if you just entrust all of them to Juingong, they will all flow into the ocean. In this ocean there is no dirty or clean; once those waves settle down, the ocean remains clear, just as it always has been.

So never think that life is pointless. It's not. Our bodies are like gloves that we put on and take off, and our foundation is like the hand that wears the gloves. The gloves don't move on their own, do they? There's something inside that moves them. It is this that we need to pay attention to. It would be wonderful to see everyone living without illness, pain, anxiety, or poverty. If you can recognize that even your suffering and hardships are flowing and changing, and if you can entrust them all to your foundation and so attain the ability to live at ease, as Hanmaum, I'll be so grateful and my heart won't ache.

Nonetheless, whether things go well or poorly depends upon how you use your mind. Further, you have to go forward being aware of both the good and the bad. Only then can light arise from within your mind. If nothing confronts you, there will be no light. So don't discriminate between good and bad, and instead inwardly let go of both sides. Then light can arise from within you. So when this light is arising from you, and arising from the members of your family, then we can truly function as one, sharing the same life and the same mind.

People go on about this religion and that religion, emphasizing what they believe, but before we speak of religion, we need to know that the foundation that sustains us—and even our life itself, including all the things we do—is already the truth. There's no need to be bound to the name of a particular religion, nor should you be led around by something that's no more than a portion of the whole. The name of the religion is just a label that developed according to a particular culture and time. When I see you lost and struggling, unable to see how things truly are, it really breaks my heart. So I can't help but to tell you what's real and what's illusion, and what we have to rely upon. I couldn't live with myself if I didn't speak out. Yet even if I didn't say anything, the truth is still there for each one of us to discover.

No matter what you do for yourselves or others, if the source of your words and actions is not deeply sincere and honest, there will be no benefit for anyone. Please think deeply about this, and shake yourself free from the names of religions. Even "Buddhism" is just a name. See the truth that underlies the names. The eternal foundation of all life is directly connected to our foundation and to everything in the world, so everything functions together as one mind.

For example, parents work so hard to raise their children, don't they? If the children ignore their parents, they cut themselves off from the energy of their parents' hearts, and life becomes difficult for all of them. So they'll need a "hand," the hand of virtue and merit, to help them embrace each other and become one. Entrusting everything to our fundamental mind, without discrimination, is itself this virtue and merit. I'm afraid I'm not very good at giving entertaining talks; I only know what's deeply true. Anyway, when you're in a desperate situation, are funny stories or movies really that interesting?

Today, I'll answer whatever questions you have. If you want to learn, you need to ask questions as well as listen. But ask questions without any thought of asking. You haven't carried your footsteps along with you, nor have you stored up within you all of the words you've ever spoken. Likewise, ask questions freely, while letting go of your fixed ideas. This is "doing without any thought of doing."

QUESTIONER 1: I deeply appreciate having the chance to ask a question. I have heard that once we die, spiritually we cannot develop any further, and that we're forced into the cycle of rebirth, into samsara, by our karmic consciousnesses. So I don't quite understand the reason for holding a *cheondo** ceremony, a ceremony that helps the dead move on. I would be grateful if you could explain to me how it is that dead beings, who have no bodies, can be helped.

KUN SUNIM: Can you see your thoughts and consciousness?

QUESTIONER 1: No.

KUN SUNIM: But they still exist, don't they? Likewise, your fundamental mind exists even though you can't see it. And it doesn't disappear when your body dies. All of our thoughts, behaviors, and everything are automatically recorded in this foundation. Those recordings will come back out sometime in the future, while what was recorded in the past is coming out in the present.

You need to know that there's no reason for you to become tangled up in endless rebirths, because the past, present, and even the future are all empty. This is why I'm always telling you to practice entrusting everything to your foundation. Right now, the record of all the good and bad we've done exists within us. Further, these karmic states of consciousnesses are unable to discern right from wrong. They come out through your brain so you mistake those for "me," and they also influence the direction of your thinking. You have to recognize these and return them to your foundation. Only then will these consciousnesses follow your intention.

Let me give you an example: when some piece of karma from your past arises within you and you entrust it to your foundation, that's like recording over an old tape. The old data is erased by the new data. When you are entrusting the situation to your foundation, it is like making a new, blank recording over an old tape. Practicing like this, you'll be able to investigate and understand everything, both inside as well as outside. Further, the karmic obstacles from your past will dissolve, and you'll know what it means to live as a true person.

Basically, it's possible for us to raise thoughts because we are alive, and of course because mind is formless. Thus, it's urgent that we practice while we are alive and have the opportunity. After we die, the good karma and bad karma we've created while alive determine the path we take and how we are reborn. Thus, while alive, we need to thoroughly understand how the way we use our minds affects us, we need to raise the level of our consciousness, and further, we need to free ourselves from the endless cycle of rebirth.

However, if we die without having cultivated our minds, we'll think that we still have a body, and so we can easily become stuck and unable to go forward on our path. Both our good karma and our bad karma will create various images that stick to us like shadows. We'll be stuck there, caught up in those images. Should we have to cross a river, we'll be held back by the fear of drowning. And when flames block our path, the fear of being burned will keep us from passing through them. All because of the illusion that we still have a body. That's why a spirit sometimes needs a guide to show it the path. That's why we hold the cheondo ceremony.

Long ago, there were two friends. One of them died, and the other friend saw the spirit of his dead friend about to enter a frog's body. The living friend shouted at him, "Hey! What are you doing?" Of course, it was only the spirit of the dead man who could hear the shout. The spirit answered, "Well, this house seems like a wonderful mansion. So I thought it would be nice to live here." Once you enter a frog's body, it is very difficult to rise above that level of existence. As you adjust to the frog's life and environment, the habits and consciousness of a frog will grow within you and lead you to be reborn in that form again. With a frog's body, how could you function at a human level of consciousness? This would make it so difficult for you to be reborn at the human level. Thus the dead often need help in order to move forward on their own path of spiritual development.

QUESTIONER 2: I've listened to a lot of your Dharma talks, but there are still so many things I don't understand. I'd like to ask you about a Buddhist monk called Zhitong, who was a disciple of Huineng. After attaining the Dharma, Zhitong wrote a verse that said, "To think that spiritual practice is done outside your daily life is foolishness. Further, 'dwelling in' or 'upholding' are also counter to the truth." Please teach me about the stage of mind to which he was referring.

KUN SUNIM: Please come over here. I'll teach it to you. Come here, closer. Here, give me your hand.

[When the questioner held out his hand, she slapped it gently with her hand four times. At first this seemed to be a slight rebuke, but as it continued, it looked more like a caring encouragement, as if she was also patting his hand. Her actions would have been seen as a statement that he was heading in the right direction but needed to be more diligent in his practice. After that, the questioner bowed to her with his palms pressed together, and she returned the bow.]

Do you understand? Now, do you have any other questions?

QUESTIONER 2: No, not right now. Thank you very much.

QUESTIONER 3: One of my friends was having some problems, where she couldn't concentrate or even remain seated for more than five minutes. So I called her to see about stopping by, but after talking for only a few minutes, she improved dramatically. Somehow, every time I called her, she seemed to improve. After several phone calls she was doing much better. It seems my practice helps other people, yet I cannot help my own son, who suffers from severe sinus infections. Why is this?

I would also like to ask another question. Sometimes friends ask me where heaven is. I tell them what I have learned from you: "Heaven is within your own mind." I say that people living with peaceful minds go to heaven after they die. But my friends still ask, "But where is it?" I once read a Buddhist book that said heaven is at a place called the Brahma realm, but this confuses me. We are told that when we have a peaceful mind, we are in heaven, yet according to that book, heaven is far off in some realm of the universe. So I don't know what to tell my friends. Although I've been coming to the Seon Center longer than they, I'm still confused about this myself.

KUN SUNIM: Rather than worrying about trying to impress others with what you know, you'd better work harder on your own practice. If you don't know for yourself, you have no business trying to answer other people's questions. Now, who told you that heaven is in the Brahma realm?

QUESTIONER 3: I read it in a book.

KUN SUNIM: There's no such thing. The Brahma realm doesn't exist separately from this world. Hell is right here in this world, heaven is here, and the Brahma realm is also right here in this world. Look at the world around us: if someone commits a crime, they go live in prison. Likewise, when you do something bad, your mind feels like a hell realm. But when you live free from the shackles of your mind, everywhere you are is a heavenly realm. Heaven and hell are not somewhere else. They are right here.

QUESTIONER 3: What will happen to us if we can't cross the river or pass through the flames after we die? What will become of us if we can't cross them at all?

KUN SUNIM: You'll reappear in this world according to your level at that point. It's straightforward: rags reappear as rags and gather with other rags; scrap metal reappears as scrap metal and gathers together with other scrap metal. Whether we like it or not, we reappear again and again with different shapes.

Earlier, you mentioned that other people got well, but not your son. Start by examining yourself. Did you teach your son how to practice? We have to be able to hold out our bowl in order to receive food.

Having faith in Juingong is holding out our bowl. You can directly reach the foundation within only when you have direct and sincere faith. It doesn't matter how long you have been coming to the Seon Center to practice. A problem like that occurs because your mind is directed outwardly. If you want to improve your practice, you need to start letting go of everything to your foundation.

QUESTIONER 3: But I've told my son what I learned from you about practicing and Juingong. He seems to have a lot of faith in this; he even saw you in a dream, but he still hasn't recovered.

KUN SUNIM: Nonetheless, there's still something wrong with his practice. Licking the outside of a watermelon can't help him know what the inside tastes like.

QUESTIONER 4: I'm excited to be able to see you today, and I'd like to ask about something you mentioned in a previous Dharma talk. You said, "The father and son are inherently not two. They need to function together as one, yet they have a hard time meeting each other. Nonetheless, they're only separated by the thickness of a sheet of paper." Could you explain the meaning of "the father and son" and "a sheet of paper," and tell us how we can break through this barrier?

KUN SUNIM: There is an eternal, fundamental mind that leads you and causes you to evolve. This is the mind that exists before thoughts arise. This fundamental mind is the "father," and the present consciousness that raises all kinds of thoughts is the "son."

For example, think of electricity as your fundamental mind, the "father," and the light bulb as your present consciousness, the "son." In order for light to arise, both the bulb and the electricity have to be there. And they have to be connected to each other. When you have faith that both the father and son are inherently connected to each other, as you act upon this faith, energy will flow back and forth between these two, and the bulb, or your present consciousness, becomes brighter. The "son" has to want to find the "father"—then they can communicate with each other and function together harmoniously.

A person being born is the result of our fundamental mind combining together with flesh and present consciousness. Everything we've done over endless lives has been automatically recorded within us and tends to gather together with those that have similar affinities. This karma, and our reactions to it, forms our present consciousness. The basis of this present consciousness exists throughout every part of our body, no matter how small.

Thus, we have to know this eternal self, which causes us to be born, and that this foundation is connected to all of the lives within our body and works together as one with them. Then we truly can know where we've come from, and where we're going, and where we are now. What I'm saying is that in order to thoroughly understand everything, you have to truly realize how your foundation and these consciousnesses are working together and manifesting.

QUESTIONER 5: This is the first time I've come here. There's something wrong inside me, and I hurt so much that I can't even sit down. One of my friends told me that you've helped many other people and might be able to help me. Please, please help me with this disease.

KUN SUNIM: I'm not a doctor, but if you diligently practice letting go and relying upon your fundamental mind, you'll know for yourself that this disease doesn't have to affect you. Even diseases react to how we use our mind. But, up until now, the lives within your body haven't been aware of this connection with your foundation. Thus there's been no room to relieve whatever is bothering you.

If your faith carries over into your daily life—if it's strong and you're diligently trying to rely upon your foundation throughout your daily life—then I'm there together with you, as well as all of the wisdom, power, and love of all Buddhas. If you're touched by this great compassion and virtue, isn't it possible that your body would return to normal? If you're very sincere about this, your condition may greatly improve almost immediately. However, if you relax your efforts and take it easy afterward, the next time something difficult arises, you won't be ready to handle it. It'll be too much for you. If you want to be able to take care of everything that arises in your life, you must continue diligently.

QUESTIONER 6: Coming here, I feel as if I have arrived in the Pure Land of Amitabha Buddha. To me you are like Amitabha Buddha, and so this place must be heaven. I would also like to ask you how I can cleanse and purify my body.

KUN SUNIM: I've told you that paradise does not exist someplace other than where we are at every moment. Even though this is a simple idea, it is vitally important. Everything depends on how you think and upon how you make up your mind. A single thought could become reality and manifest into this world. A single thought could cause you to fall into hell. And a single thought could cause you to be reborn in heavenly realms.

Also, Amitabha Buddha is not separate from your fundamental mind. Aksobhya Buddha, Amitabha Buddha, Avalokitesvara, and Ksitigarbha are all manifestations of our fundamental mind. All of these are just different names for Buddha, for one mind. This is why we believe in and rely upon Buddha, and practice returning everything and gathering it together in one place.

Tell yourself, "Only Juingong can take care of my body. Even if it's time for me to die, Juingong can help me die without pain—just like when beans are ripe, they easily come free from the pod." It's Juingong, our true self, that can help us die without pain; it's Juingong that can truly show us the way; it's Juingong that can help us evolve so that we may be reborn with a higher spiritual level in our next life; and it is Juingong that can lead us to higher realms. Therefore, you should practice diligently.

QUESTIONER 6: I felt so wonderful after I came to the Seon Center for the first time that I decided to give entrusting a try. But when I do this, it feels like my head might...

KUN SUNIM, smiling: Thank you for working so hard. But you're trying too frantically to entrust. You don't need to force it. Your true nature is already with you. Everyone born into this world already has this foundation complete within them. You're here, so your foundation is also here. So just trust that and relax. And whether you're awake or asleep, sitting or standing, doing this or that, know this: "Ahh, Juingong, you're here; you're the one who's taking care of things." Just trust this foundation and turn everything over to it. This is entrusting.

QUESTIONER 6: Thank you.

QUESTIONER 7: I'm grateful for this opportunity to ask you a question. Actually, I'm so nervous in front of all these people that I realize just coming up here and asking a question has been good practice for me!

These days there is a strong preference for work that doesn't involve manual labor; it seems as if people want to avoid difficult things. Could you say something about this preference?

KUN SUNIM: You should accept whatever comes to you. Don't try to avoid what's coming, nor try to cling to what is leaving. Always harmonize yourself with the truth; let go of your worries, and move through life naturally.

QUESTIONER 7: Who created Buddha?

KUN SUNIM: All sentient beings did.

QUESTIONER 7: Do we make our thoughts, or do they just spontaneously arise?

KUN SUNIM: They're neither created nor do they just arise.

QUESTIONER 7: It's often said that "I" doesn't exist, but if that's true, then what is this that's speaking to you now?

KUN SUNIM: It's said that "I" doesn't exist because in all the things we do there's no trace of a fixed and unchanging "I." When you came here, did you carry your past footsteps with you? You just walked over here; there wasn't some fixed consciousness involved in each step. Speaking is like this too, isn't it? Nothing is fixed or unchanging.

QUESTIONER 7: Thank you.

QUESTIONER 8: Whenever I used to have difficulties, I could usually resolve them one by one by entrusting them to Juingong. However, when too many hardships happened all at once, I was overwhelmed. So I asked you about this and after practicing as you suggested, I was able to take care of everything. I feel so grateful for your guidance, and I'm trying to entrust even this gratitude to Juingong.

I've heard people speak of "giving back," or "returning the merit," when we finish something we've been working on, or succeed at something. So I was wondering if there's any special way we have to entrust or let go in order to make this happen?

KUN SUNIM: You've been taking care of things and entrusting the results, and even entrusting the gratitude you feel, so what else is there for you to do? Keep practicing as you are, and continue entrusting even your gratitude. Then the blessings of your practice will naturally shine on everyone around you.

QUESTIONER 8: Thank you.

QUESTIONER 9: Thank you for this opportunity. In one sense, there are so many things I want to ask about that I don't know where to begin. I've been coming to Buddhist temples for almost twenty years, and I've been here about five times. Yet despite this, my faith doesn't seem very firm.

My mother passed away when I was young. At that time my uncle, a minister, became a source of guidance and inspiration for me. He took me to church and tried to persuade me to adopt Christian beliefs. But no matter how hard I tried, I couldn't feel any faith in Christianity. Jesus said, "Follow me, and you will be saved." But I found it difficult to accept that idea. In fact, it strongly repelled me. It left me with the feeling that religion was just something created by human beings. On the other hand, what the Buddha said—"Do not follow me, follow the Dharma"—seemed right to me.

However, even after attending Buddhist temples for a long time, I wasn't able to develop any particularly deep faith in Buddhism either. Then two months ago I read a book of your teachings and felt like you explained so much! Although I didn't start practicing in the way that you teach, it seems to me that I've already been living my life in accord with your underlying meaning. I'd like to think I've already been living by relying on this deep, fundamental mind.

If one doesn't follow a particular religion, but tries to live in accord with the fundamental meaning, can one still draw upon the unlimited and mysterious power that you say all human beings are endowed with? If so, is there any difference between living like this and going to Buddhist temples or studying what you teach about relying upon one's fundamental mind?

There is another point I'm concerned about. It seems like awakened people must be very detached. However, since I was born a human being, I would like to be able to fully respond as a human being: feeling sad, happy, or irritated when those kinds of things arise. So I'm hesitant about jumping into practice, and I wonder if it would be possible to practice without having to make the Seon Center or a temple the focus of my life? I'm confused and have little faith. Could you please teach me about this?

KUN SUNIM, laughing: I think you need to pay a bit more attention! Okay? Listen: Buddhism and your life aren't separate. The first syllable of the Korean word for Buddhism, *bul*, refers to the everlasting foundation of life, and the second syllable, *gyo*, refers to everything communicating and working together. Thus, the word *bulgyo*, Buddhism, describes our lives. To put it another way, the lives and activities of all things are, in and of themselves, the Buddhadharma. Our daily life itself is fundamentally one mind, and truth itself. Buddhism is not something separate from our daily life. How could Buddhism and daily life be separate from each other?

QUESTIONER 9: I see. So it sounds like it's not necessary for people to come to the temple. They can just practice at home.

KUN SUNIM: Then why do you send your children to school?

QUESTIONER 9: Thank you. I'll try harder.

QUESTIONER 10: Kun Sunim, I have a fiancé whom I really love, but we always seem to be fighting. He's a soldier and has a soldier's attitude, so I find myself getting easily irritated. In fact, the doctor said my thyroid gland isn't functioning well, so I don't know if that's why I get so angry, or if the anger has caused my thyroid problems. Anyway, how can my fiancé and I get along better and become one?

KUN SUNIM: In general, it's best if couples have similar ways of thinking. However, even if they don't, you and he can still get along if you're a bit wiser in how you handle your thoughts. Still, it will be very difficult if there's a huge difference in the way you two think. The most important thing is this: rather than worrying about "becoming one," you need to have faith in your foundation and entrust it with everything; you need to know that "My foundation is leading me." Do you understand?

Don't give in to your temper so easily. More than anything else, losing your temper affects your health and ruins your body. Do you know why this is? The moment you lose your temper, each and every consciousness within you also loses its temper, and this causes your body to break down. It really does happen this way.

QUESTIONER 10: Thank you.

QUESTIONER 11: I was waiting downstairs and summoned my courage to come up to the Dharma hall. Currently all of my family is practicing entrusting and letting go to Juingong. My mother has been a diabetic for many years. Her eyesight had greatly deteriorated, and she also had surgery and was bedridden for a long time. Then a couple of months ago, she began entrusting everything to Juingong. Since then, she hasn't needed insulin injections or any other medications, and her condition has greatly improved. I've felt deeply grateful and told many others about this wonderful practice.

A few days ago, however, she fell in the bathroom. When that happened, I thought to myself, "Even this can be used for practice. Entrust it to Juingong." However, my mother is still in a lot of pain, so I am not sure whether I entrusted all of this in the right way.

KUN SUNIM: You're doing just fine. But there's something else you should know. You have to let go of both sides, both living and dying. Balance and harmony will be lost if you force a dying person to stay alive. The moment you let go of both sides, light will burst forth. If you are afraid of your mother's death and try only to keep her alive, this is not the way of truth. You won't be able to realize the true meaning of one mind. Gather up your faith and practice letting go of both sides. Then how could your efforts not bear fruit?

QUESTIONER 11: Thank you. I will practice harder.

QUESTIONER 12: My brother-in-law had a stroke when he was twenty-six, and he is now thirty years old. He has two little children and seems just too young to be disabled like this. I've felt bad for my brother-in-law but have been caught up in my own stuff. I suddenly realized that I should have come to ask you about his situation much sooner. I think I've been diligent about practicing with my own situation, but I realized that I never really thought about entrusting my brother-in-law's condition. And now he's started attending a church. This made me realize I needed to start talking to him about your teachings, telling him that God is within him, and be sure to pray inwardly. However, his condition hasn't improved.

As I was coming here today, it occurred to me that if he had been my child instead of my brother-in-law, I would have come and asked for your help almost immediately. I feel bad that I wasn't able to help him and so he wound up going to a church.

KUN SUNIM: This Buddhadharma, this great sun, shines on everything without distinction. It shines on those who are doing well and those who aren't. It's just that people have blocked this light. Do you understand? This applies to your brother-in-law as well. This fundamental mind of ours is so important. You have to return inwardly—take everything and return it back to this one place. When you gather everything in this one place, the energy that arises from that can lead you and take care of your body. As a result your health will improve. However, how can this happen if someone doesn't work at doing it, doesn't have faith in it?

People shouldn't hate or disparage themselves, for within them is the guide that leads them. So tell your brother-in-law to keep returning everything to that one place at least until his body recovers. This truth encompasses everything, because everything has life. So how can it be split apart into "Buddhism" or "Christianity?" It's because people use their minds so narrowly that they can't escape from their suffering.

QUESTIONER 13: Last night I saw you in a dream. I've been in a lot of pain lately, and in the dream you said, "Let's give it a try!" I prayed all night and was finally able to briefly fall asleep. In a dream, I heard a voice say, "Grab hold of his ankle." I don't understand this at all. I know it's just a dream, but...

KUN SUNIM: It's just a dream, but at the same time, it's not just a dream. Everything depends upon how we determine to see things. Because you make up your mind a certain way, you have certain dreams, and because you have certain dreams, you can make up your mind that way as well. So beginning with how you think, have firm and calm faith, sincerely let go of everything and go forward. This is the meaning of "grab hold of his ankle."

QUESTIONER 13: Thank you. I will do this.

KUN SUNIM: Everything in the world is like this, so be at ease and go forward. Completely give everything to your foundation and step forward into your life.

There exists
neither the Buddha realm
nor the universe,

neither the four types of life
nor the four seasons,
neither the east nor west,
nor time,
neither emptiness
nor even nothingness.

There is no place
without wind, water,
and the blossoms of flowers.
There's no place
that isn't vibrant and alive.

The mountains that came before,
the mountains still to come,
transforming
and manifesting,
freely coming and going
without the least movement.
Yet feet remain feet
and hands remain hands.
So incredible, so incredible!

[With this, Daehaeng Kun Sunim stepped down from the Dharma
seat.]

Mind: Treasure House of Happiness

SUNDAY, DECEMBER 18, 1994

EVERY ABILITY IS ALREADY WITHIN YOU, WAITING TO BE USED

I feel sad when I see so many of you standing outside in the cold because the Dharma hall is too small to accommodate everyone. At the same time, I am deeply touched that, despite the uncomfortable conditions, all of you have gathered here together to practice spiritual cultivation.

As you know, all living creatures in the world, whether animal or human, have different physical shapes and spiritual levels, and each has its own special characteristics. For example, horses have sturdy hind legs, and cows have horns. It is so amazing how nature has endowed each living being with its own unique shape and ability.

Likewise, we human beings have been endowed with the ability to take in through the senses everything in the universe, to process it, and then send out whatever is needed, whether it is from the material realm or the realm of mind. It is due to this ability that,

---

once we are born as a human being, it's said that we already have ninety-nine percent of what it takes to become a Buddha. Through mind we have the ability to digest everything and then send out whatever is needed. But there are a lot of people who can't do this, because even among human beings there are so many different levels of spiritual development.

Have you ever thought about the computer that people use to control a robot? Without the computer, a robot can't move at all. If we compare the human brain to the computer, then the body is the robot. The function of the brain is to integrate everything that's received from the outside, to process it, and then send out the appropriate response. And it is mind, our foundation, that sends the orders to the brain.

However, a computer can only operate a robot according to the specific instructions it has been given. Unlike a computer, the human brain is able to process whatever it encounters and respond spontaneously to any circumstance. This brain is vastly more powerful than any computer in the world. People often think that they can't do something because they lack the ability or because they're hindered by previous bad deeds. But they should completely ignore thoughts like these. Why? Because once you're born as a human being, it doesn't matter whether you've been a human being for a thousand lives or for one day—the inherent functioning of everyone's brain is exactly the same. So don't get caught by ideas that something is easy or too difficult. It is you who creates thoughts such as "can" or "cannot." Fundamentally, "can" and "cannot" do not exist. This formless mind of yours isn't hindered by anything, nor is its functioning dependent upon anything else.

Throughout the entire universe there is a fundamental, infinite energy upon which all things depend. The ability and potential of every single thing in the universe arises from and returns to this energy. Regardless of what else people think, or how things may appear, everything is continuously functioning like this. Every single thing continuously revolves around this fundamental energy, transcending time and space. Wouldn't it be nice if you could let go of everything and just flow with this energy? This mind we have is formless—it can freely go anywhere, it's able to think of anything, and it can respond to whatever arises. We are all endowed with such vast, unimaginable ability, so sometimes I really can't understand why some people think they're stuck and can't move forward.

IT IS MIND THAT FREES MIND

It is mind that can free mind. It is also mind that hinders itself, saying, "This can't be done." What tells you this are the thoughts that were input in the past. It's these thoughts, which have accumulated within you over eons, that are the source of what are sometimes called defilements and delusions. These thoughts have accumulated within you one after another and will eventually manifest one by one, according to circumstances. How, then, can you free yourself from these thoughts? If you can just leap over those thoughts, everything will be fine. You have the ability to do this, but most people don't make the effort to use it.

Several years ago, there was a man who went bankrupt because he had guaranteed someone else's loan. One day, he received a notice from the bank demanding that he pay off the loan, and he was consumed with anger and fear. Finally he became sick. When he came to see me, I told him, "That money wasn't originally yours. Now you have to decide whether you're going to continue clinging to those feelings about that money, or whether you're going to let go of them. Since the money itself is already gone, wouldn't it be better to let go of those feelings as well?" If he could accept the fact the money was already gone and let go of the thought that he'd lost it, he'd feel much more calm and peaceful. And he would have a chance to make a fresh start. However, if he couldn't let go of the thoughts about his losses, he wouldn't be able to recover his health or his business.

I told him, "Your money is already gone. To tell you the truth, you're the one who made it possible for your money to disappear. It's already gone, so what is there to hang on to? If you keep clinging tightly to things that are already in the past, then that state of clinging will be continuously recorded in your brain. This will cause the consciousnesses of the lives within you to stagnate and become more negative. The result is that your body won't function properly, and your ability will deteriorate." If you understand how this works, then you'll realize that this is one of the most powerful and fearsome principles of the human realm.

Therefore I advise you to generate thoughts wisely. If you input a better thought, the previous accumulation of negative thoughts will be replaced with the new data. When you raise a thought, it passes through the cerebrum and the cerebellum and goes to the middle of the brain. The middle part of the brain evaluates the thought and sends the response to all parts of the body. This is not just a description of a biological process. It's something that you have to know how to use for yourself in your daily life. When you are sick, you may need a doctor's help, but there's a limit to how much a doctor can help you. In most cases, other people can help you with only twenty or thirty percent of your problem; you have to do the rest of the work by yourself. It may seem like my talks aren't much fun, but I have no choice, because it is so urgent that you understand this process. How long can your body last?

THE FOCUS OF OUR FAITH

People often talk about faith, but let's be clear about where the focus of your faith should be. Your foundation is something that no one else can give you or take away. In the end, who is the one that can truly help you when you are in need? Who will soothe your pain? Who will rescue you from poverty? Who will take care of you when you're suffering or dying? Ultimately, only your foundation can truly take care of all of these things.

Just as a computer has the programming necessary to control a robot, your brain possesses all of the ability to move your body. All of the ability is there, waiting to be used. The brain, our own computer, is fully endowed with the five subtle powers, which the brain can use to process everything and to send out what's needed. It is our fundamental mind, our foundation, that enables the brain to use the subtle powers latent within it.

Therefore the Buddha said, "Whom do you believe in? Above all else, discover your true self, your Juingong. It is intrinsic within you, so it has to be discovered within you." It's good to see so many of you working to believe in and uncover your true self, but it seems to me that you should think more deeply about what you need to do in order to find your true self.

People often say that they are so busy they don't have time to look for Juingong, or that when some disaster occurs, they can't pause long enough to entrust their circumstances to Juingong. And yet, it is Juingong that leads the brain and allows it to make use of the five subtle powers that are inherent within us.

So we each have to rely upon our own foundation. If you entrust everything you face to your foundation, then what you have entrusted—that is to say, what you have input—is recorded into your foundation. It's as if your foundation notices that you are starting to rely upon it, and so it responds to you. Then the results of what has been input will manifest in your life. However, if you try to depend upon something outside yourself, no connection is made with your foundation, and so nothing is input into it. If nothing is input into your foundation, how can it take care of things? Thus the Buddha said that no matter what you do, unless you rely upon your true foundation there would be no virtue and merit in your actions.

People often ask why they aren't enlightened, even though they have been following the Buddha's teachings for a long time. But it's because they are too drawn toward outside things in their daily life. Whether you live as a monk or a layperson, you must rely on your inner self, honestly and devotedly, and produce results through your own efforts, without hoping that someone else will intercede for you. Does true happiness come from someone else? Does true freedom come from someone else? No one can give you happiness and freedom, and no one can take them away either. No one else can take your place when it comes to these things. Ultimately, you are the one who takes care of yourself.

It's so important to continue entrusting everything in your life to your foundation, because how you live in this life determines what kind of role you can fulfill in your next life. Look at how actors and actresses approach their roles in plays. They try to understand their particular role and do their best to play the role they have been given. After the curtain falls, having finished what they had to do, actors put down their burdens and feel at ease. Although their characters may have died on the stage, they go home in good spirits and relax. Think about this.

In the same way that actors take on roles in a play, you came into this world and took on a role according to how you had lived in your previous lives. However, even though you received the role of a beggar in this life, if you continuously entrust everything in your life to your foundation and do your best to live sincerely, then later you will be able to receive a better role. This is actually happening everywhere around us. If you think about this, you should have some feeling for where you came from, where you are going, what you are doing, and why you are doing it.

Everybody knows that if you plant beans, you will harvest beans, and if you plant rice, you will harvest rice. The body you have in your next life and your role in it will depend upon how well you've fulfilled your current role, upon how well you've lived. Have you seen in the movies how a person who lived a bad life falls into a hell filled with snakes and animals when she dies? This doesn't happen only in the movies. Everything about how you live is automatically input into your foundation, and this causes you to be reborn at the level that matches your behavior. For example, although someone had a human body in her previous life, if she lived at the level of a snake for most of her life, she will be reborn with the body of a snake when she reappears in this world. We've each gone through so many different lives, and lived with uncountable different shapes. So how could there be some creatures that we could look down upon? How could your life be precious, but not that of an animal? Every single life is your life, and every single shape is your shape.

Everything that people are experiencing now is the result of what they've done in the past; there's not some separate place where they're punished. If they behave like a snake, they will reborn as a snake. If their behavior is at the level of a cow, they will be reborn at the level of a cow. If they lived at the level of an insect, then their spirit will end up taking the form of an insect. That's hell itself!

Sentient beings have been living like this for so long, without knowing the truth. However, Buddha—which is the foundation of everything in the universe, of all visible realms, unseen realms, and the principles by which they function—exists everywhere at all times, and through cause and effect and the cycle of rebirth, helps every single thing in the universe to develop. The mind of Buddha manifests as uncountable Bodhisattvas, which help everything function. Thus it is said that Buddhas and Bodhisattvas are not separate. For example, if we describe Buddha as the fundamental energy, then Bodhisattvas are the energy that is produced by this fundamental energy. That energy, which has arisen from the foundation, goes on to become the fundamental energy of something else; this process repeats itself again and again. This is the way our universe is functioning.

It may seem like I'm repeating myself, but everyone must absolutely know this point: everything in the entire universe, including the past, present, and future, functions together as a complex, vast, and diverse whole. Given this, how should we lead our lives? How can we become one mind, Hanmaum, such that all hands become our hands and all bodies become our body? Even though a thousand drops of rain fall on the ocean, they all become one with the ocean. In this way, if you put the minds of all things and all living beings into Hanmaum, they all naturally become one mind, one hand, and one body. When everything becomes one like this, this itself is Buddha. After those minds become one with Hanmaum, they manifest as different energies; we call these energies Bodhisattvas. These Bodhisattvas fill the world around us.

When we flip a switch, the electricity flows and the light comes on. In this same way, when you entrust something to your foundation, your mind becomes one with Hanmaum, so whatever energy is needed flows freely. This energy that flows out is what we call

Bodhisattvas. We give it different names according to how this energy manifests. For example, when somebody is sick this energy manifests as the Medicine Bodhisattva, and when somebody is suffering this energy manifests as the Bodhisattva of Compassion. Although Bodhisattvas have many different names, they are all manifestations of the same foundation. It's like this: when a man sees his wife, he becomes a husband; when he sees his parents, he becomes a son; when he sees his children, he becomes a father. Buddha, the source of everything, has infinite manifestations, so sometimes it is called the Diamond Throne.*

YOU CAN TRULY KNOW ONLY THROUGH APPLICATION

So far today, you have only listened to these teachings: you still have to apply them. Earlier, when a sunim brought me some rice cake, I told her, "Taste it, and tell me if it's any good." So she replied, "How can I know for sure whether you'll like it or not? You'd better taste it for yourself." Like this, you have to take what you've heard about practicing and wholeheartedly apply it and try to experience it for yourself. Only then can you truly know what it tastes like.

Listening to lectures or understanding theories is not enough. When I meet people who think that they understand everything, sometimes I just silently look at them because they are so full of theories that they can't hear what I would say to them. Rather than talking about theory, one single step can take you all the way around the universe. For example, when someone in your family is sick, entrust it to Juingong and observe with firm belief. In cases where the disease is caused by karma, the cause must be dissolved in order for the disease to be cured. When you entrust it to Juingong, the record of what was done in the past dissolves, and so the current suffering also dissolves. So if you truly entrust everything to Juingong, then, without your even being aware of it, time and space are transcended and the suffering that confronts you begins to dissolve. But just superficially repeating "Juingong" won't help you a bit.

Someone complained that her situation wasn't improving even though she entrusted everything to Juingong. She said that when she first started entrusting things to Juingong, they turned out well, but as time went on, it seemed like entrusting things didn't work anymore. Listen, after graduating from middle school, you must go on to high school. How can you grow if you don't go to the next level?

When you're traveling, there are times when you have to get off the bus before you reach your destination, aren't there? Nonetheless, sometimes people think of getting off the bus as a failure. But if you look at it from a positive perspective, such as "Even getting off the bus was done by Juingong, so Juingong will make sure that things work out for the best," then because that situation was input positively, things will turn out okay; there will be nothing to worry about. So when you're finished with what you have to do, just get on another bus. It only takes an instant to change your thoughts. However, some people may spend several days or even months clinging to the same thoughts before they are able to continue along the road. There is a saying, "Both success and failure are the path." Why do soldiers retreat on a battlefield? In a bad situation, isn't retreat also a strategy to save the lives of soldiers?

Our lives are so complex, aren't they? Likewise, our bodies are also very complex. Our bodies contain such an intricate web of nerves and other cells, and the brain contains so much that's beyond knowing. Using this system, the foundation sends orders through the brain to the different parts of the body and makes them move. Even more amazing is the functioning of the spiritual realm, the invisible realm; it is truly indescribable how things change and manifest after they have been input into Hanmaum.

However, the only way to know this for yourself is to directly touch it, taste it, and put it into practice. Picture a wireless microphone. If you've never used one before, you won't know how to turn it on or test it. However, as you keep trying to use it, you'll eventually understand how it works. Likewise, unless you put your understanding of Juingong into practice, it will be hard to make progress in the cultivation of mind or in the matters of your daily life. Never forget that you also have the ability within yourself to improve even your country through the thoughts you give rise to.

THE PART WE HAVE TO DO OURSELVES

There's one more thing about this that you need to know: we can raise mind to help those people around us, but there are some parts that they themselves have to do. If they aren't trying to rely upon their foundation, the problem will still remain, because some fundamental part of it hasn't been taken care of. Thus, in order for people to completely solve their problems, they have to know how to entrust, observe, and experience for themselves. This is why I'm always telling you to teach your children about this practice.

Even if the Buddha were to solve all of your problems, it would only be a temporary relief. It wouldn't help you the next time a similar problem or hardship arose. You'd still suffer because you hadn't learned how to work with your foundation to take care of these things. Nobody else can live your life for you. Even when troubled people receive a lot of help, in many cases their lives don't improve, because their perspectives and behaviors continue as before.

This is why the Buddha taught people to entrust everything to their foundation. Everything! He said, "If you do good things, you will receive good results, and if you do bad things, you will receive bad results. However, people intent upon developing further should try to let go of all discriminations between good and bad because the things that are considered as good and bad are fundamentally not two. So they both exist within you, and unless you abandon these, even though you try to do only good things, you will also commit harmful actions. Although you try to cause harm, you will also unconsciously do good deeds. When you truly understand the fundamental nonduality of all things, and let go of dualistic thoughts such as good and bad, then you can become a Bodhisattva and a Buddha."

Everything is done by your foundation, the ability of which is inconceivable. The realm of human beings—the middle realm—functions together with the upper realm and the lower realm. If we can transcend the habits of this middle realm, and live attuned to the upper realm, then we'll be free of the trap of Earth-type thinking and we can experience true peace. When this occurs, everything will be different. However, in order to achieve this, we must transform ourselves. As you practice, changes will happen naturally. Start with little things and experience what happens when you begin entrusting them to your foundation. If you take your body and your daily life as materials to practice with, then later you will reach the stage where your mind can encompass the entire universe. When such minds begin to radiate outwardly, when they begin to radiate and function faster than even the speed of light, everybody will naturally become one and this world will become a Buddha realm. It will become a Buddha realm where everyone lives grounded in their fundamental mind, free of attachments, desires, and fears.

Does anyone have any questions?

QUESTIONER 1: Each time I listen to your teachings, I feel ashamed that I have not been practicing hard enough. On the other hand, I'm grateful because each time I listen to one of your Dharma talks, I feel a bit more of my ignorance peeling away.

I'm a professor of physics. Today I was surprised during your Dharma talk because you answered all of the questions that I intended to ask. But I would still like to ask you anyway in order to confirm my understanding. I talk about your teachings with my students, so I want to make sure that my understanding is correct.

When I hear you say that everything is constantly changing and manifesting every instant, I think of how an atomic particle changes its orbit and of the energy that is produced as a result of this change.

Also, when you say that karmic consciousnesses, ignorance, and delusions hinder us and decrease our ability, I think of this in medical terms, as when someone's circulation is restricted, causing them illness and pain.

Kun Sunim, there is something else I've been wondering about. You often compare our fundamental mind to an automatic computer. However, in this world, when we want to communicate with someone far away, we have to dial a number, and in order to listen to the radio, we have to tune in to a frequency. What about when we entrust everything to Juingong? Is the frequency automatically tuned in?

KUN SUNIM: Yes, it's automatic. As you know, using any machine such as radios, phones, or robots involves all kinds of fine tuning and adjusting. However, when you truly entrust things to your Juingong, then, one after another, the automatic computer that is your brain takes care of absolutely everything. While a regular computer can output only what's been input, the brain possesses infinite and inconceivable abilities; it automatically processes all inner and outer signals and communications. Not only this, it also processes everything that arises from our foundation. So if you raise a thought, then it's like that thought pushes a button. It is done automatically and unconsciously. However, do you realize what most people are doing? They may push the button, but then they give up and release it right away. People keep giving up as soon as they push the button. If I compare the act of completely entrusting something to pushing a button most people put their finger on the button but then don't push it all the way. Time after time, they keep doing this: because it wasn't completely entrusted, nothing was transmitted, so how can anything be done about it?

Everything depends upon the decisions you make. So would you ignore the foundation that leads you and instead believe in someone else? If you won't believe in your own root, what else would you believe in? Would you trade your foundation for the empty sky or a statue? Once, when I was frustrated at how people were living, I spoke as simply as I could about the mind of all Buddhas. This was later used as a song: "The Buddha's form and my form are not two. The Buddha's mind and my mind are not two. The teachings of the Buddha are all contained within the daily life of all beings." Our daily life is Dharma itself. Our daily life is the Buddha's life. It doesn't exist separately from us.

Things in the material realm happen the same as they do in the realm of mind. Everything is constantly transforming. From a basic state, particles are generated, and then these eventually gather together and create more particles. These gather and continuously transform, and eventually form a universe. And this universe itself eventually returns back to the basic state, which eventually again forms a new universe. This process repeats itself again and again, and is so incredible. The energy it generates is beyond imagination. The universe, the human brain, and mind all work in exactly the same way: if you think bad thoughts, harmful seeds will radiate outward far and wide, and if you think good thoughts, seeds of goodness will spread out endlessly.

This is why even a single thought can be so important. When you help others by giving material things, it's relatively insignificant. It's only a drop in the ocean. If you really want to help others, then help them through mind. Most people would like to help others, but if they're not careful in how they raise thoughts for others, those thoughts can spread outward and harm small or weak things. If we don't help other people develop their minds and deepen the level of their spiritual development, the loss to our countries, the world, and the universe will be truly unimaginable. Although good and evil exist in about equal proportions, the evil is much more intense and active. So those harmful seeds are spreading faster throughout the world, and in a thousand different ways.

QUESTIONER 1: I've heard you compare Juingong to a column of fire. Can I assume that this column of fire means the place where all energies and all minds merge together?

KUN SUNIM: When you entrust everything to Juingong, then all energies instantly gather together. Everything spontaneously comes together, separates and scatters, and comes together again; this takes place in the invisible realm, but it can also manifest into the phenomenal realm as well. For example, the aspect of coming together is like government officials reporting an important matter to the president. The aspect of splitting apart is similar to the president making a decision and giving the officials their instructions. However, this is as far as the comparison goes. Relying upon Juingong is far more powerful and effective. Once you entrust something to Juingong, everything is taken care of spontaneously. It works like a computer, processing things automatically.

Just as pushing a button on a computer can give you all kinds of information about someone, if through your own experiences you truly understand how this principle of one mind works, then as easily as pushing a button, you can know how you lived in the past. However, if others don't know how Hanmaum works, it's not right for you to tell them what their past life was like or what their future will bring. Telling people things like that is contrary to the path, because through mind, through just one thought, everything can be changed. Try to experience for yourself how a single thought entrusted to your foundation can transform the things in your life.

You can apply this principle to every part of your daily life, according to your level of spiritual development. So no matter whether the things you face are big or small, don't be afraid of any of them. Don't be overwhelmed; stand up to them courageously and go forward. Even if the sky were to collapse and you could see no way out, you should still be able to smile at it all. If you've reached this stage, you could hold up the sky with one finger. Such a level of mind is so wonderful and precious. You may wonder how a finger could support the sky, but the finger that can truly hold up the sky is not a material thing that can be described—it is mind.

QUESTIONER 2: I am a member of the Busan branch of Hanmaum Seon Center. I run a small business, but it's not going very well. Because of the problems with my business, I have difficulty maintaining my practice. So I'm here to ask for your guidance and your compassion. I'm frustrated now. I haven't been studying for long. Although I keep struggling to practice, my frustration continues. Sometimes I wonder if it's because the power of my Juingong is weak.

KUN SUNIM: Juingong isn't weak, your faith is. Why aren't you trying to rely upon your Juingong?

QUESTIONER 2: That didn't come out quite right... I practice earnestly, but—

KUN SUNIM: Look! All things are being done by our foundation. So if you are truly entrusting it with everything that arises, what is there that can't be taken care of? Who is running your business? It's you, right? Actually, though, you're just running errands on behalf of the business, aren't you? The real owner is your Juingong, the captain within you who oversees all of the lives in your body. It's the captain that is running your business, and it's the captain that's guiding you. Do you understand?

QUESTIONER 2: I'm afraid I misspoke before...

KUN SUNIM: The one that causes you to move is the master within; your body is not the master. Your body is like a planet, where many different beings live together. "You" don't exist by yourself. Right now in your body there are so many different consciousnesses, shapes, and lives. Even when you drink a cup of water, you don't drink it alone. Rather, all the lives in your body drink the water together; they all live together, sharing everything. The same principle that applies to your body also applies to your business. A business functions because the owner, the manager, and the employees all pitch in and work together. You should know that, "it's not me that's doing all these things, it's Juingong. I'm just running errands, together with everyone else." View things like this, and you will truly understand.

QUESTIONER 2: I don't think I expressed myself well... I would like to ask if you could raise a thought for my business so that it will go well.

KUN SUNIM: When you truly entrust everything you face to Juingong, when you're wholeheartedly pressing the button, everything instantly combines together and becomes one. Without any hindrance everything gathers together, and Juingong evaluates it, makes a decision, and sends out instructions. So there's nothing to worry about. Truly and sincerely entrust your situation, and it will be taken care of like that. It doesn't matter whether the problem is big or small. The owner of your business is your Juingong, so sincerely believe in your Juingong and entrust everything to it.

QUESTIONER 3: Kun Sunim, I came here from Pohang to express my deep appreciation to you for teaching me about Juingong. I'm a beginner who encountered your teachings about a year ago. I'm married and have a son and a daughter. After ten years of hard work, I'd saved enough to buy a wonderful three-story apartment building. However, my husband had previously guaranteed a loan for his brother's business, which went bankrupt. As a result of this, the court placed a lien on my building for 180 million won. After all our hard work and saving, I was heartbroken and in despair when I realized that we would lose the building without having even lived there.

To my surprise, I felt no hatred toward my brother-in-law, instead I felt sympathy for him, and thought, "Well, Juingong, my brother-in-law was trying to do his best." After discussing it with my husband, we visited my brother-in-law and told him that we would sell the building if he needed us to. My brother-in-law was so grateful when he heard this. And we also felt happy and at peace because we had entrusted everything to Juingong: "It was Juingong that caused my husband to guarantee his brother's loan. So it is Juingong that will minimize the loss. Solving this quickly also depends upon Juingong." In this way I've been continuously entrusting everything to Juingong. If I hadn't known about this practice, I think my anger and frustration would have ruined my health. Moreover, it was such a traumatic situation that my husband and his brother could easily have become enemies. Kun Sunim, thank you again for teaching me how to raise a warm and compassionate mind. I would also like to thank the sunims of the Pohang branch. I will do my best to practice as diligently as I can.

KUN SUNIM: Making up your mind like that and releasing everything is good for you. It prevents you from becoming ill, and it lets you be at peace. Sometimes our life may seem too hard to endure, but good things will naturally come to you because your mind has become broad and rich.

QUESTIONER 3: Kun Sunim, thank you!

KUN SUNIM: Don't worry! Everything will be okay.

QUESTIONER 4: First of all, I would like to thank you for teaching us about Hanmaum, about one mind. One day you mentioned that if beings can't adapt creatively to the times they live in, they would regress or even perish. In this context, is Korean Buddhism regressing or progressing? And what does the development of Korean Buddhism depend upon?

KUN SUNIM, laughing: Ultimately, it is mind. What else would it be? I've looked carefully at Korean Buddhism as well as other religions. A tree lives relying upon its own root, and like this, each one of us also has to rely upon our own root. However, so many people are seeking "The Lord," "God," and even "Buddha" outside of themselves. What kind of virtue and merit can result from ignoring the fundamental energy that is the source of all things? What kind of awakening, what kind of development can arise from that? Some limited material advancement may be possible, but nothing more. There must also be spiritual development. Only then will the hindrances to development disappear; only then will unlimited spiritual and material growth be possible. Also, it is through mind that we can keep the world from falling into confusion. It is only because of the functioning of mind that the Earth, planets, and universe are able to function properly. All of these are things that only mind can take care of.

All of the cruel things in the world—murder, lying and swindling, not caring about one's neighbors, thinking only of one's own benefit, and in general behaving like an animal—all of these happen because people use mind in wrong ways. People do these things because they don't truly know themselves, nor do they know their capabilities or their role in life. Likewise, people are easily cheated and often fail because they don't know the limits of their own ability. Let's compare a person's ability to a bowl. When we know the size of our own bowl, then we can put things into it according to its capacity. If we don't know our own capacity, and put a large amount into a small container, most of what we try to put in will overflow and cause problems. Therefore, when you do something you should first truly know yourself and your capacity, and then go forward while entrusting everything to Juingong and observing. If someone tries to swim across a river without knowing his own ability, he may drown before reaching the other side. Many people borrow a lot of money in order to start a business, but due to the interest, their burden increases with each passing month. It would be better to earn a simple living and spend less than to incur a lot of debts. If you overreach yourself, you may lose your house or even fall into poverty.

QUESTIONER 4: Would you tell us something about the influence and role of Buddhism in postindustrial society?

KUN SUNIM, pointing to her chest: If you know your own capacity and believe in your root, while knowing that all energy originates from your root—if you put all of this understanding into practice in your daily life, you will realize that you are connected to the whole of existence. Everything is your business, your pain, your family, and your body. So there's nothing you can treat carelessly. And those practitioners who cultivate mind have to be especially cautious not to be careless about anything, because their mind is connected and communicates with every mind in the universe, all the way from Buddhas and Bodhisattavas to insects. If you reach the stage where you can communicate like this, your mind will become one mind with everything. When you can communicate with everything like this, then even if a life-or-death situation confronts you, everything will become one mind, and hands that aren't hands will fill the air and help you. It's just so amazing! At this point the whole world would become a Buddha realm!

QUESTIONER 5: I'm honored to meet you. This is the second Dharma talk of yours that I've attended. Also, I'm reading your book *The Principles of Hanmaum** for the second time. The more I read it, the deeper it resonates within me, as if you were speaking directly to me. Kun Sunim, I will continue to practice wholeheartedly with the firm belief that through this practice all of my karma will melt away and my family will live harmoniously. Kun Sunim, there are many people around me who live in misery. If they knew about this practice, they too could be free from their suffering, couldn't they?

KUN SUNIM: Please explain to them how to entrust and observe.

QUESTIONER 5: I've already been explaining it to them.

KUN SUNIM: If you entrust and observe while explaining this to them, then I'll also be there with you and so will all Buddhas.

QUESTIONER 6: I am a member of the Seon Center's youth group. Somebody once said that in South Korea alone almost a million people are either possessed by spirits or are influenced by them. I've seen some of this myself, so I know it can happen. Further, it seems that the family of someone who is under the influence of spirits has a lot of problems and is not very harmonious.

For a long time I've been wondering why some people are influenced by spirits. I've noticed that the more intelligent a person is, the more prone he or she is to be affected by spirits. Among young people there are many who graduated from prestigious universities but who are now wandering around in the mountains praying and trying to obtain supernatural powers from various spirits. I've heard about many of these cases and have witnessed some of them myself. When I see those who are possessed by spirits, or are in contact with them, it also seems that their families are full of conflicts. Is there some kind of family karma that's the cause of both things? Also—

KUN SUNIM, smiling: May I say something now?

QUESTIONER 6: I was just wondering how the family's karmic affinity relates their problems with—

KUN SUNIM: Yes, I understand. There are three types of circumstances that lead to problems with spirits. First, if one's parents or ancestors worshiped certain spirits, then those spirits may remain connected to members of that family. Second, when someone dies in a car accident or drowns, most of the time the person's spirit can't leave the place where he or she died. You would think that a spirit could go anywhere it wanted to, but often it can't move even an inch away from the place where the person died. In those cases the spirit can leave only after someone else's spirit replaces it. This type of situation can cause a lot of problems.

Third, all of the information about how you have lived in the past, including your thoughts, feelings, and behaviors, along with the lives and shapes you've had, are completely recorded within you. In some cases these karmic consciousnesses manifest and claim to be certain spirits; people can be deceived by these consciousnesses into thinking that they are possessed. These consciousnesses will seem like insane spirits that are possessing them. This is why, when something like this happens, raising even a single thought well is so important. Otherwise, your body can become a puppet. First one consciousness forces you to do something, and then another consciousness orders you to do something else, and then yet another consciousness causes you to do something different.

This happens time after time, and even causes you to do things harmful to yourself or others. People who see how you're acting will think you're insane.

To solve problems caused by spirits, you can't just try to get rid of the spirits, you have to help them move forward from the level they're stuck at. To do this, you have to become one with them through the foundation. Imagine that there are three drops of water. If you put them into a cup of water, the three drops all become one with the water. Likewise, by returning them to your foundation, you and those spirits can become one. In becoming one with the foundation, those spirits are freed from the fixed ideas that are keeping them from moving forward. You may have to do this once, twice, or even three times until they all become one cup of water. When this happens, everything will be okay.

However, there may be other ways to help spirits. For example, a long time ago a mother who had two young children suddenly died. Sometime afterward her husband tried to remarry, but strange accidents kept happening to each woman he considered marrying.

After he told me his story, it occurred to me that rather than just helping the dead wife's spirit move on from this realm, it would be best if the minds of the first wife and the new wife could be combined together as one. With a bit of wisdom and flexibility, a way can be found that benefits everyone. There's a saying that when parents have wisdom, the children will turn out well, but if the parents lack wisdom, the children tend to have problems. Let's think about the situation from the perspective of the wife who died. She was raising her children with so much love, and just as it seemed like her family's hardships were over, she suddenly died. Imagine how heartbroken she must have felt. After helping the minds of two wives become one, you wouldn't believe how happy and harmonious their family became!

When a judge evaluates a case, he examines the circumstances surrounding the event and people, and given those circumstances he asks himself what the best solution might be. In this way, when sunims hear about problems with spirits, they have to ask themselves what would be the best for everyone involved. For example, they need to reflect upon the nature of the person's suffering, their economic situation, their family circumstances, and the spiritual levels of everyone involved. For sunims, sincerely entrusting everything to their foundation is the basic thing they have to do, but in addition they also need to be able to manifest and respond appropriately to the problems that people bring to them. Sunims should ask within themselves what they need to do to truly help others, and what things they should be aware of in order to properly guide people. This should be how a sunim lives. Of course, even among sunims there are so many different levels.

Let me give you another example of ways to help spirits. There are some cases where spirits are so vicious and deluded that they don't respond at all to compassion or love. For instance, if these kinds of spirits were very greedy in their pursuit of material things while they were alive, people have to show them a lot of paper cut in the shape of money and large amounts of other material things in order to guide them. Problems with spirits can also arise if people die suddenly. Their spirit may not be able to leave the place where they died, and so they unknowingly cause a lot of problems to occur at that spot. Also, sometimes they're drawn to a close, living friend, and accidentally cause her or him a lot of problems.

People have problems with spirits because they tend to believe in and search for things outside themselves. If someone is very inquisitive and focused on outside things, he may appear to be intelligent, but his tendencies make it easier for spirits to enter him. To spirits, it's as if the body is empty, as if it has no owner, so they decide to live there.

Like the patriarch Linji* said, if you don't maintain a strong, centered mind and don't believe in your Juingong, if you don't raise your Jujangja,* if you don't deeply center yourself, and instead just wander around outside, you make it easy for all kinds of spirits and germs to enter and live in your body. That's how these kinds of things happen. This is why I'm always telling you not to seek outside of yourself. Also, you should remove everything that your parents worshiped, so that those things don't negatively influence your children or their children.

In the case of problems caused by consciousnesses that arise from within, those are the results of what you've done in the past, either in this life or in previous lives. You can dissolve these by returning them one by one to your foundation, as they manifest.

Ultimately, everything depends upon mind, upon your foundation, so this practice of learning to rely upon your foundation is absolutely indispensable. However, people who are possessed by spirits or disturbed by karmic consciousnesses arising from within have a hard time letting go and observing because they are continually being harassed by these things. They are constantly being ordered this way and that: "Go there! Do this! Don't do that! Don't leave the room! Don't eat!" These things cause them a lot of hardships, and it's difficult for them to live a normal life. In cases where the family can't endure such behavior, I tell them to hospitalize the person and to calmly and diligently entrust everything to Juingong and observe.

QUESTIONER 6: I understand that I've taken up a lot of time, but I would like to quickly ask you one more question. This question is similar to my previous one. When parents are possessed by spirits, both the parents and children suffer. It appears as if the children's suffering is caused by their parents, but is it actually the result of the children's own karma?

KUN SUNIM: Yes. Like the beads of a mala* or a rosary, there is a thread that connects them all.

Please listen carefully. Have you ever noticed how cans are put with other cans? It happens naturally: cans are gathered together with cans, gold is displayed with gold, scrap iron is piled up with scrap iron, and rags are placed with other rags. In the case of human beings, politicians get together with politicians, and artists with artists. In this way, members of a family gather together because of their similar levels of awareness and their similar karma. Because of their similar karma, they experience similar things. But don't misunderstand me. What I'm saying about levels of awareness has nothing to do with people's outward shape or appearance.

However, if you have some faith in what I've taught you, if you don't allow yourself to be deceived by the consciousnesses that arise from within, if you entrust all of those back to the one place they came from, and if you have confidence that everything will be taken care of by that one place, then it won't take even a day to solve your family's problems. But a lot of people aren't doing this. Even though I have spoken about this many times in various ways, they still don't get it. What can I do? Can I go to the toilet for you? If I could eat and thereby relieve your hunger, I would. If I could save you from dying by dying myself, I would do it. But it just can't be done.

QUESTIONER 6: You mean that some children suffer the same things as their parents because they have created karma that is similar to their parent's karma?

KUN SUNIM: Yes, they have created similar karma. Parents and children tend to gather together because they have similar levels of awareness and similar karma. Thus you can't blame anyone else. Parents can't blame their children, and children can't blame their parents.

QUESTIONER 6: Thank you, Kun Sunim.

KUN SUNIM: Even though the children don't behave in the same way as their parents, the problems caused by their similar karma still remain. However, if even one person in a family practices diligently, they can dissolve that karma. But if you are the only person in your family who practices, you have to practice twice as intensely as other people; you have to go straight in, without allowing yourself to be distracted. You have to entrust everything that you and your family face to your Juingong. And if everyone in your family practices like this, then it's possible for all of your family's problems to melt away.

In any event, I am grateful that so many of you have gathered here together in order to cultivate mind. In this complex world, while living with your families and the complications of daily life, and all of the hardships of the body—to see all of you making such efforts to practice makes me think that each one of you has almost become a Buddha. Thank you.

QUESTIONER 7: I feel that in both Buddhism and Catholicism, people's faith in an absolute being leads them to become true human beings. Therefore I feel no resistance at all toward Buddhism. I feel comfortable coming here, as if I were visiting my neighbor. Just like Western people often prefer to eat Western-style food, and Koreans enjoy eating Korean food, someone who is drawn to Buddhism follows Buddhism, and others, like me, who are drawn to Catholicism, follow Catholicism. No matter which path we follow, I believe our purpose is to become true human beings and to share our love with each other. My question is this: Can a person be saved only by believing in Buddhism or can someone like me, who believes in Catholicism, also be saved? I'm really curious about this.

KUN SUNIM: That's a good question. When I traveled abroad, I attended many gatherings and discussions with people from all faiths: Muslims, Catholics, Protestants, and Tibetan Buddhists, among others. It seems to me they are all talking about the same thing.

For example, look at the Korean word for Buddhism: Bulgyo. The first syllable, *bul,* refers to the fundamental source of every single life, including even a blade of grass. The second syllable, *gyo,* refers to learning from each other; we communicate with each other through speech, intention, and mind, and through this communication we are able to listen to each other and to learn from each other—this is the meaning of *gyo.* So the word "Buddhism" is also an explanation of the truth itself. It's a description of how the entire universe functions. Thus, it actually applies to everyone and everyplace. No matter the religion, its essential teachings are that the foundation of everything exists inside, not outside.

When I went overseas and talked with Catholics and Protestants, they were saying the exact same things that I'm telling you. Regardless of religion, all sages have taught the same thing: "If you place your faith in other people or things outside yourself, you'll fall into a pit of demons. Know yourself first. The foundation is within you. Your body is a ship, and the captain is taking care of all of the lives within it. That captain is your true self. More important than anything else is knowing this true source, this true doer, because everything in the universe is connected to it. Everything in the universe functions together as one and is directly connected to your foundation, so if you know only this true source, you will be able to understand the workings of the entire universe."

However, many people, both Christians and Buddhists, are seeking outside of themselves, saying, "Oh, Lord! Oh, Buddha! Please give me this, please do that." I'm not criticizing a particular religion; I'm simply saying that you need to know your own true foundation. Regardless of your religion, you have to know your own self. No matter whether you feel worthless or confident, the truth is that because you were born into this world with a physical form, other people exist and other religions exist. Without you, nothing exists. You wouldn't be aware of any of this if you didn't exist. So know yourself first! I hope that you will think about this carefully.

There are so many beings living within your body, with so many different consciousnesses and shapes. Nonetheless, there is the master within, who takes care of all of these. This master, the captain, is the one who can balance both the material and spiritual aspects of the lives within your body, and it is this captain that takes in and sends out every kind of thing. This captain can also be called "Lord" or "Buddha." However, the problem is that people are searching for the Lord and for Buddha outside of themselves, although both are already within each of us. That's why I keep talking about this.

I don't distinguish between religions, but people behave as if they were different. The Lord is within you. Religions may have different names, but their foundation is the same. Jesus said, "Believe in me and follow me," but he wasn't telling people to believe in and follow his flesh. Originally he taught that each person should believe in his or her own inner true master. But I guess there may have been an editing problem.

Of course, Buddhism isn't exempt from these kinds of problems. Even though the Tripitaka* is filled with the truth taught by the Buddha—that you have to search within yourself—many people misunderstand the meaning of this and seek outside of themselves, or practice solely for the sake of obtaining worldly benefits. These kinds of problems have plagued every religion.

Even temples have encouraged this kind of behavior. For example, when the early Chosun dynasty began to persecute Buddhism in around 1400 CE, many monks and nuns were forced into the deep mountains. In order to survive, they sold prayer services, offered fortune telling, and sold all kinds of talismans to block evil influences. Even today some temples are still doing these things. These kinds of things tend to direct people's attention outward, away from their inner foundation. These practices should have been changed as the era developed, but they are still carried on in many places.

QUESTIONER 8: Some people say that salvation occurs through the power of a supreme being, but are you teaching that salvation is done by each person's inner, true self? Also, I have a question about cause and effect, and karma. Hearing so many people talk about their suffering, I keep wondering if it is, indeed, a blessing to be born as a human being. I understand that in order to be born as a human being one has to accumulate a lot of virtue. I think this is why it's said that humans are higher life forms than animals. But actually, in some aspects it seems like animals behave better than a lot of people do. Animals don't kill to greedily accumulate more than they need.

Also it's said that the suffering someone experiences in this life is the result of what he or she did in the previous life. It seems to me that although rich and powerful people must have accumulated a lot of good karma to be able to live so well, they seem to just waste it by doing so many bad things. This seems like such a vicious cycle: accumulate good karma and experience a good rebirth, only to fall back into painful realms, and then go through this cycle over and over. I know that some rich people live upright lives, but in general it seems that those who have the most are the ones who behave the worst. Anyway, people say that being reborn as a human being is a blessing, but is it really? That seems hard to believe.

Also, from a layperson's point of view, sunims could be considered unfortunate, because we laypeople can eat and sleep when we want to, but sunims have to live austerely, in most cases without much sleep.

KUN SUNIM: Your question nicely sums up what we've been discussing today. First of all, just believing in a certain religion doesn't guarantee that you'll be saved. Second, no matter your religion, you must know that your root [pointing to her chest] is your own true master, and so place your faith there. If you believe that everything is being done by your true root, without looking for God or Buddha outside of yourself, then you will be saved by yourself. It's you who saves yourself.

Salvation doesn't come from somewhere else. You are the one who makes your salvation and you are the one who saves your body. It's the master within, your foundation, that takes care of this collection of lives that's called a body. Because the foundation guides and directs the lives that make up the body, we often call the body a servant or an attendant. Your own root is the master, so what else is there that could give salvation or take it away? You are the one who causes yourself to be saved and you are also the one who can cause yourself not to be saved.

Did you say that sunims seemed more unfortunate than the lay-people? But that's a limited view of things. One hour of sleep can be just as restful as a full night's sleep, if you entrust the thought that it should be so. Therefore, you don't have to feel bad for them.

You also said that the cycle of birth and death seems like an endless cycle of suffering? Actually, it's not such an illogical, vicious cycle.

Did you also say that animals seem to behave better than humans, and that rich people seem to do many more bad things than ordinary people? You're only seeing a part of things. If you saw the whole picture, you wouldn't make those kinds of assumptions. Everything that everyone has done in the past is perfectly recorded within their foundation, and will return to them in due course. There's no one else who judges your behavior and determines whether you will be punished or rewarded. Everything you've done is recorded within you, so the results arise from within you. If you have lived a good life, good things will return to you; if you once kicked a beggar or treated him with contempt, you will undergo the same bitterness that you made him suffer.

Thus, to help us escape this continuous cycle, the Buddha taught us to free ourselves from both sides of all dualities such as good and evil. For example, when people help someone else, they often think that they've done something good. However, if you help someone, you will receive something, and if you receive something, you will have to give something. This happens automatically. However, if you cling to ideas such as giving or receiving, gaining or losing, this will lead to a long chain of discriminations, such as "like," "dislike," "gained," "lost," and so on. You have to let go of all of these discriminating thoughts. Only then will it be possible for you to transcend this middle realm.

Listen, I'm not trying to force anyone to do this; it isn't something that I could force you to do even if I wanted to. The reason I keep telling you about spiritual practice and relying upon your fundamental mind is because this is what you have to do in order to free yourself from the cycle of birth and death. And when you suffer, I hurt as well. Do you understand what this means?

Every kind of life gathers and lives together with others according to its level of awareness, and according to the time and place that best suits its development. All beings live like this; even on other planets, they're living like this.

As you go through your life, it takes a lot of effort to become aware of your true self, so do you really have time to judge and criticize other people's behavior? If you know and believe in your true self, you will obtain the ability to take care of everything that confronts you. Moreover, you have to continue to develop what you discover, until you are able to take care of everything in the entire universe, so how could you have time to worry about what others are doing? When you understand that nothing is separate from you, there is no need to worry about or chase after outer things. So don't worry about what other people may be doing.

However, sometimes there are laypeople who constantly examine how well sunims are doing, and there are even some sunims who make a lot of discriminations about the spiritual level of individual laypeople. But don't do that. It has to be unconditional! You have to let go of both sides unconditionally. Whether someone's wrongdoings are serious or not, they were done because of ignorance. So let go of all your preconceptions about their wrongdoings. When you let go, it had to be completely unconditional. Otherwise, it's not letting go. Even among those you think of as rich, there are so many miserable and pitiful people. You complained about rich people doing many bad things, but sooner or later they will have to experience the consequences of their actions.

The same principle applies to giving. Suppose you gave a hundred dollars to the temple. You'd know how much you gave, right? Likewise, if someone gives me some money, I know who gave it to me and how much it is, don't I? The awareness of those facts doesn't disappear; it is all automatically recorded within your foundation. So don't get caught up in thoughts such as "I donated some money," or "I helped someone." I also never think, "His situation improved because of my help." It's not "me" that does those things. It all happens naturally when we rely upon our true nature.

However, if sunims spend offerings wastefully, if they treat those offerings casually because they didn't have to earn them through their own sweat and toil, or if they gather large sums of money, and live in luxury, or buy land and houses, all these behaviors will be input into their foundation. These kinds of sunims are worse than worldly people.

Every single behavior is recorded within our foundation. Nobody can escape from this. Everything is recorded exactly as it is. Thus, a life built on deceit will come to nothing. Such people have no idea of the harmful seeds they're planting, nor do they even realize that truth and sincerity are completely missing from their lives.

However, sunims who have diligently practiced relying upon their fundamental mind live freely, without clinging to anything. If someone feels sorry for those sunims and gives them some money, although the sunims receive the offering, there is no moment of receiving or using it. Why? It's because even though those sunims receive something, they don't dwell on any thoughts of having received something, and even though they give something, they don't dwell on any thoughts of having given something.

Laypeople also should live without clinging. For example, if a friend or relative is in a desperate situation and begs you to lend her some money, if you actually have the money, just give it to her unconditionally. Just give her the money without worrying about whether she will pay you back. Why? Because if you give the money with the expectation of being paid back, then later, if you can't collect the money, your friendship may fall apart and in the end you may become sick or even die. Some people even try to profit from their friends' or relatives' hardships by charging them high interest rates. Unwise thoughts like these cause people to suffer life after life, and their children also suffer because of this lack of wisdom. So from the very beginning, give it unconditionally.

Let's stop here for today.

Thank you.

Afterword: The Mind of All Buddhas

The mind of all Buddhas is my one mind.

The wisdom of all Buddhas is
the wisdom of my one mind and daily life.

The body of every Buddha is
the body of every sentient being.

The love and compassion of all Buddhas is
the love and compassion of all sentient beings.

Doing good or doing bad,
all depend upon how I use my mind.

—Daehaeng Kun Sunim

Glossary

Avalokitesvara: The Bodhisattva of compassion, who hears and responds to the cries of the world, and delivers unenlightened beings from suffering.

Baizhang: A master who lived in China from 720–814 CE.

Bodhisattva: In the most basic sense, a Bodhisattva is a manifestation of Buddha that helps save beings and also uses the nondual wisdom of enlightenment to help them awaken for themselves.

Buseol: He was born in the Silla Kingdom of Korea, probably around the year 610 CE. He was ordained at Bulguk Temple and spent more than a decade living on Duryun Mountain with his Dharma brothers Yeonghi and Yeongjo. After many years of practice, the three of them left for the Odae Mountains (sometime during the reign of Queen Seondeok, 632–647 CE.). While traveling, they spent a night at the house of a layman, in what is now the district of Mangyeong, in North Jeolla Province. It was there that the incident with the layman's daughter, Myohwa, took place. Buseol married Myohwa and they had two children, a son and a daughter. Although married, Buseol continued to practice diligently and achieved enlightenment before either of his Dharma brothers.

Cheondo: This involves helping the consciousness of the dead to move forward on their own path. It can happen that beings become "stuck" in their fears, attachments, and illusions and so can't move forward. Cheondo often involves a special ceremony that in a sense educates the consciousness and so allows it to move forward at a level that more accurately reflects the level the person achieved while alive.

Diamond Throne: This sometimes refers to the place where Shakyamuni Buddha was sitting when he realized enlightenment, but it also refers to our unwavering, fundamental mind.

Hanmaum: Pronounced "han-ma-um." "Han" means one, great, and combined, while "maum" means mind, as well as heart, and together they mean everything combined and connected as one. What is called "Hanmaum" is intangible, unseen, and transcends time and space. It has no beginning or end and is sometimes called our fundamental mind. It also means the mind of all beings and everything in the universe connected and working together as one.

Huineng: Dajian Huineng, a monk, was the sixth patriarch of Zen Buddhism in China, and lived from 638 to 713 CE.

Hwadu (C. hua-tou, J. koan): Traditionally, the key phrase of an episode from the life of an ancient master, which was used for awakening practitioners, and which could not be understood intellectually. This developed into a formal training system using several hundred of the traditional 1,700 koans. However, hwadus are also fundamental questions arising from inside that we have to resolve. It has been said that our life itself is the very first hwadu that we must solve.

Ignorance (無明): Literally this means "darkness." It is the unenlightened mind that does not see the truth. It is being unaware of the inherent oneness of all things, and it is the fundamental cause of birth, aging, sickness, and death.

Juingong (主人空): Pronounced "ju-in-gong." *Juin* (主人) means the true doer or the master, and *gong* (空) means "empty." Thus Juingong is our true nature, our true essence, the master within that is always changing and manifesting, without a fixed form or shape. Daehaeng Kun Sunim has compared Juingong to the root of the tree. Our bodies and consciousness are like the branches and leaves, but it is the root that is the source of the tree, and it is the unseen root that sustains the visible tree.

Jujangja: Literally, the staff that monks used to carry. In the context of Seon, it also refers to the mind that is centered upon its foundation.

Karmic consciousnesses: Our thoughts, feelings, and behaviors are recorded as the consciousnesses of the lives that make up our body. These are sometimes called karmic consciousnesses, although they don't have independent awareness or volition. Sometime afterward, these consciousnesses will come back out. Thus we may feel happy, sad, angry, etc., without an obvious reason, or they may cause other problems to occur. The way to dissolve these consciousnesses is not to react to them when they arise and instead to entrust them to our foundation. However, even these consciousnesses are just temporary combinations, so we shouldn't cling to the concept of them.

Kassapa, or **Maha Kassapa:** Regarded as the foremost of the ten great disciples of the Buddha. He was well known for his self-discipline, and the Buddha himself praised Kassapa for his attainment and realization. After the Buddha's passing, Kassapa was chosen to lead the great council that gathered to record the teachings of the Buddha.

Ksitigarbha Bodhisattva: The guardian of the earth who is devoted to saving all beings from suffering, and especially those beings lost in the hell realms.

Linji (J. Rinzai): Linji was one of the greatest Chinese Chan (Zen) masters and is considered the founder of many of the modern branches of Zen. He died in 866 CE.

Manjusri: The Bodhisattva who represents the essence of wisdom. Manjusri is traditionally portrayed holding the sword of wisdom in his right hand, and in his left hand he holds a blue lotus that represents the flowering of wisdom, while riding a lion that represents courage and majesty. In temples and paintings, he is often together with Samantabhadra.

Mind (心; K. maum): Not the brain or intellect, but rather something intangible, beyond space and time, and without beginning or end. It is the source of everything and everyone is endowed with it.

Nujin (漏盡通): This is the state where one is free of all the things that cause suffering, where one is never caught by any thing or situation. It is also described as the state where one is not caught or entangled by even the five subtle powers, and so one is able to use them freely, as needed.

One Thought: This refers to the ability to raise and then input and entrust a thought to our foundation. When we can connect with our foundation like this, then through our foundation that thought spreads to everything in the universe, including all of the lives in our body. At that instant, because all things are fundamentally not two, they all respond to that thought.

The Principles of Hanmaum: This is a collection of Daehaeng Kun Sunim's teachings that was published in English as *No River to Cross: Trusting the Enlightenment That's Always Right Here* (Wisdom Publications, 2007).

Samantabhadra: The Bodhisattva who represents the enlightened application of wisdom in the world. Samantabhadra is usually portrayed as riding a white elephant and helping the Buddha educate and save unenlightened beings. He is often paired with Manjusri.

Seon (J. Zen): Seon describes the unshakable state where practitioners have firm faith in their inherent foundation, in their Buddha-nature, and so return everything they encounter back to this fundamental mind. It also means letting go of "I," "me," and "mine" throughout daily life.

Sunim / Kun Sunim: Sunim is the respectful title of address for a Buddhist monk or nun in Korea, and Kun Sunim is the title given to outstanding nuns or monks.

Tripitaka: The canon of Buddhist scriptures.

Vimalakirti: A lay disciple of Shakyamuni Buddha who was renowned for the depth of his enlightenment. His name means "pure" or "unstained." He appears in the Vimalakirti-Nirdesa Sutra, where he taught even the great disciples of the Buddha. He is portrayed as the ideal layperson, one who attained the essence of the Buddhadharma and who thoroughly applied his understanding to his life. He would help those who were poor and suffering, and teach and educate those who were behaving badly.

Index

Page numbers in bold indicate glossary definitions.
Page numbers followed by "(2)" indicate two references.

parent–children rifts, 91, 142

See also faith in true nature...; inputting thoughts into our foundation; letting go; relying on fundamental mind...

evil spirits, 67–68, 69–70

evolutionary power of mind, 59–61

experimenting with experiences, 3–4, 13–14, 34, 51, 74–75, 84–85, 124

F

faith in true nature/true self/ fundamental mind/foundation, 1, 12, 26–27, 31, 33–34, 34–35, 50, 115–20

and illness (disease), 63–64, 66, 71, 78–79, 97–98, 99–100, 106–9, 120–21

See also entrusting what comes up to...Juingong; inputting thoughts into our foundation; letting go; relying on fundamental mind...

falling into emptiness, 12, 35

family problems, 78, 135–36

among parents and children, 91, 141, 142

practice and, 66–67, 134–35, 141, 142

father and son image, 98

finger supporting the sky image, 128

five subtle powers, 13, 80–81, 84

freeing yourself from, 13–14

fixed ideas, 83–84

letting go of, 57, 61–62, 78–79, 92

forward progress. *See* progress in practice

foundation. *See* fundamental mind

fundamental mind (foundation), 6, 11, 12, 19–20, 20–21, 31, 43, 44, 74, 92–93, 99, 113, 115, 120, 122

discovering. *See* discovering your true self

faith in, 26–27, 31, 34–35, 50, 115–20

inputting thoughts into, 78, 81–83, 83–84, 85, 86–87, 114–15, 116, 125–26, 160

relying on/entrusting what comes up to, 4, 9, 19, 22, 24–25, 26–27, 31, 42, 49–52, 78–79, 87, 99–100, 104–5, 108, 116–17, 122–23, 139–40, 148, 150

See also Hanmaum; Juingong; true nature

fundamental questions, 10–11, 99, 117

furnace image, 3, 44–45, 52–53

G

gateway within, 14

girl's dream story, 67–70

giving: letting go of, 53–54, 149–51

glove and hand image, 90

good and bad: letting go of, 90, 123

gratitude, 12, 49, 71, 72, 103

graves in Korea, 55–56

Manjusri, 76, **159**
  and Vimalakirti, 74–75, 77
masters. *See* awakened masters of old
"me". *See* "I"
meditation, 73
mind (maum), 18, 57, 113, **159**
  cultivating. *See* practice
  functioning of, 126–27
  misuse of, 80, 133
  one mind. *See* Hanmaum
  power. *See* power of mind
  spirits and, 57
  as unlimited, 79, 84, 112–13
  and world problems/destruction,
    61–62, 67–70
  See also fundamental mind (founda-
    tion); thoughts
"The Mind of All Buddhas" (Daehaeng Kun Sunim), 153
money
  giving, 149–51
  loss of, 114, 130–32

N
negative thinking, 5, 18, 82–83, 112–13
nonduality, 44, 123
  letting go of dualistic thinking. *See*
    under discriminatory thoughts
  of the living and the dead, 55–57
  of ourselves and others, 5, 6, 76–77
not killing, 85–86
not worrying, 23, 44–45, 50–51, 53,
  57–58, 82–83, 106, 148–49

Nujin, 81, **159**

O
observing and going forward, 3–4,
  6–7
one mind. *See* Hanmaum
One Thought power, 59, **160**
others
  becoming, 14–15, 15–16
  criticizing, 5, 148–49
  helping, 66–67, 91, 127, 138;
    beings/lives within the body, 63,
    71, 74–75, 160
  nonduality of ourselves and, 5, 6,
    76–77
  praying for, 30
  regarding as yourself, 46–47
  saving, 10, 26–27, 52

P
parents and children
  karmic similarities, 140–41
  problems among, 91, 142, 141
the path, 9, 14, 16, 21
perfection process, 15–16
positive thinking, 4–5, 82, 121–22
  and illness, 84, 114–15
power of mind, 112, 113, 128, 133
  evolutionary power, 59–61
  One Thought, 59, **160**
  See also five subtle powers
power plant image, 11–12, 44
practice (spiritual practice)

Saha world, 25

salvation, 146–47

Samantabhadra, 15, 76, **160**

saving others, 10, 26–27, 52

schizophrenia: treating, 84

See also hospitalization

secrecy re experiences of self-
discovery, 12–14, 17, 128

seeking outside yourself, 23–24, 132,
139, 144, 145

See also praying to someone/
something...

self

consciousness, 99. See also karmic
consciousnesses

discovering. See discovering your
true self

knowing yourself first, 26–27,
33–34, 133, 143, 144

praying to someone/something
apart from yourself, 29–30, 34

regarding others as yourself, 46–47

seeking outside yourself, 23–24,
132, 139, 144, 145. See also praying to someone/something..., above

See also "I" ("me"); true nature (true
self/Buddha-nature)

self-references of Daehaeng Kun
Sunim, 21–22, 82, 83–84, 90, 91,
113, 120, 141, 148

Seon (Zen), **160**

spirits

the dead and the living, 55–57

evil spirits, 67–68, 69–70

helping, 79, 94, 137–39, 156

and mind, 57

problems with, 79, 135–37, 139,
140–41

See also karmic consciousnesses

spiritual development. See progress in
practice

spiritual practice. See practice

starting with yourself. See knowing
yourself first

stuckness of the dead, 94

subtle powers. See five subtle powers

suffering

ending, 63, 108–9

ignorance as the cause of, 6, 73–74,
79–80, 133

See also difficulties (problems)

sunims, 64–65, 66, 86, 138, 146, 147,
150, **160**

supreme beings, belief in, 21

T

teachings

applying, 120–22; practicing the
teachings of Daehaeng Kun
Sunim, viii, 5

of the Buddha, 21, 116(2), 123, 148

of Buseol, 45–46

of true self, 13

teachings of Daehaeng Kun Sunim

essentials, viii, 1, 2–5, 6–7, 89

hand-slap teaching, 95

Also by Daehaeng Kun Sunim from Wisdom Publications

———————

NO RIVER TO CROSS
Trusting the Enlightenment That's Always Right Here
Foreword by Robert Buswell

"*No River to Cross* speaks directly and simply from the heart, much in the manner of Shunryu Suzuki's *Zen Mind, Beginner's Mind.*"
—Francisca Cho, Georgetown University,
translator of *Everything Yearned For*

Anyang Headquarters of Hanmaum Seonwon

(430-040) 101-62 Seoksu-dong, Manan-gu, Anyang-si
Gyeonggi-do, Republic of Korea
Tel: (82-31) 470-3175 / Fax: (82-31) 471-6928
www.hanmaum.org/eng – onemind@hanmaum.org

About Wisdom Publications

Wisdom Publications is the leading publisher of classic and contemporary Buddhist books and practical works on mindfulness. To learn more about us or to explore our other books, please visit our website at wisdompubs.org or contact us at the address below.

Wisdom Publications
199 Elm Street
Somerville, Massachusetts 02144 USA

We are a 501(c)(3) organization, and donations in support of our mission are tax deductible.

Wisdom Publications is affiliated with the Foundation for the Preservation of the Mahayana Tradition (FPMT).